Make It, Gift It

HANDMADE GIFTS FOR EVERY OCCASION

by Mari Bolte

CAPSTONE YOUNG READERS
a capstone imprint

Table of Contents

From Me To You: Handmade Gifts for your VIP

Pretty Packages

Make It, Gift It!

In a world of craft blogs, activity sites, and Pinworthy projects, finding inspiration for personalized gift-giving has never been easier. But it can also be overwhelming. Where to begin? Take the first step to finding and creating the perfect gift for the special people in your life.

Be prepared for any event with *Homemade Holiday!* From traditional holidays to graduations, sporting events, or the changing of the seasons, there's a great gift to give.

Paint Chip Calendar, page 12

Eco Gifts is full of ideas for the gifter on a budget, the eco-conscious, and the innovative! Custom candles, fluffy flowers, and dinky jewelry are just the start.

Books 'n Birds, page 60

Give gifts that come from the heart directly to the stomach with *In Good Taste*. Home-baked bread, festive fruit bouquets, and sliceable cookies make sweet treats for any occasion.

Fresh Fridge Pickles, page 78

From Me to You is full of ideas to brighten someone's day. From simple stationary, gift card holders, or hand-sewn mittens, you'll find a Very Important Present for the Very Important Person.

Sendworthy Stationary, page 100

5

Wrap It Up

Gift giving starts with the packaging! Dress up even the most simple gift with these simple yet stylish wrapping projects.

Simply Wrapped

What You'll Need:

gift

wrapping paper

clear tape

1. Remove any tags or labels from your gift. (Especially the price tag!)
2. Measure the wrapping paper so it overlaps when folded over the gift. The sides should overlap slightly when folded toward each other.
3. Center the gift upside down on the wrapping paper. Wrap the paper around the gift and gently pull until tight. Secure with tape.
4. On one side of the package, fold the ends of the wrapping paper toward each other. Firmly crease around the box's edges. Crease the triangle-shaped flaps. Repeat on the other side of the package.
5. Fold down the top flap, creasing the top edge. Fold up the bottom flap, creasing at the bottom edge. Secure with tape.
6. Pinch two fingers together and run them along every edge of the gift. This will create a crisp fold.
7. Finish your gift with a ribbon. Cut the ends of the ribbon at an angle for a prettier presentation.

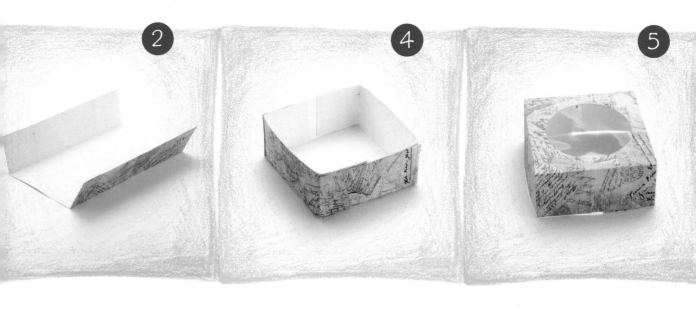

To Go Box

What You'll Need:

two 8.5 square inch (54.8 square centimeter) pieces of cardstock

clear plastic, such as a sandwich bag or transparency paper

1. Crease each side of the cardstock two inches from the edge. Make two cuts at the top of the cardstock and two at the bottom.
2. Fold in the side creases. Tuck the corner flaps inside the creases and secure with tape. This is the bottom of your box.
3. Repeat steps 1 and 2 with the second piece of cardstock to make the box's lid.
4. Cut a circle in the center of the lid.
5. Trim and tape a piece of clear plastic to fit over the circle.
6. Place the lid on the bottom of your box.

Shake It Up

What You'll Need:

sold-colored gift wrap

clear cellophane

confetti

1. Wrap your gift in solid-colored gift wrap.
2. Wrap the gift in cellophane, leaving one end open. Do not wrap as tightly as the wrapping paper.
3. Sprinkle confetti between the wrapping paper and the cellophane. Shake gently to make sure confetti falls between all the cracks.
4. Tape the open end of the cellophane shut.

Nothing is worse than wondering how you're going to wrap a funny-shaped gift! This custom-sized gift bag is here to save the day.

What You'll Need:

wrapping paper

clear tape

1. Figure out how much wrapping paper you'll need. You will need enough to cover the entire gift.
2. Fold the wrapping paper so the edges meet in the center. Tape in place.
3. Fold the bottom of the bag up. This will create the base of the bag. Make sure it's wide enough to hold your gift.
4. Open the flap of the bag's base. Fold so the outside edges touch. Tape in place.
5. Fold the top and bottom corners in so the tips of the corners touch. Tape in place.
6. Place gift in the bag and tape to seal.

Homemade Holiday

Gifts for Every Occasion

Bring gifts for birthdays, holidays, special events, or just because! Never arrive empty handed with this collection of gifts suitable for any event.

12 PAINT CHIP CALENDAR

14 HAPPY BIRTHDAY!

Paint Chip Calendar

Help your friends and family stay organized in the new year with this easy-to-make, easy-to-use calendar. Paint chips, scrapbook paper, or even photographs make great days of the week.

What You'll Need:

large frame

ruler

paint chips

rubber cement

binder clip

Velcro dot

microfiber cleaning pad

ribbon

dry erase marker

1. Remove the mat from the frame. Decide how large of a margin you want around your calendar, including space at the top for the month. Lightly mark the margins on the mat with a pencil.
2. Cut 35 paint chips to fit between the margins, in five rows of seven. Allow for a little extra space between each chip.
3. Glue chips to the mat. Let dry completely.
4. Replace the mat in the frame. Write in the month, days of the week, and dates.
5. Attach the binder clip to the calendar with a Velcro dot. Use the clip to hold the microfiber cleaning pad.
6. Tie one end of the ribbon to the dry erase marker. Tie the other end to one of the binder clip's handles.

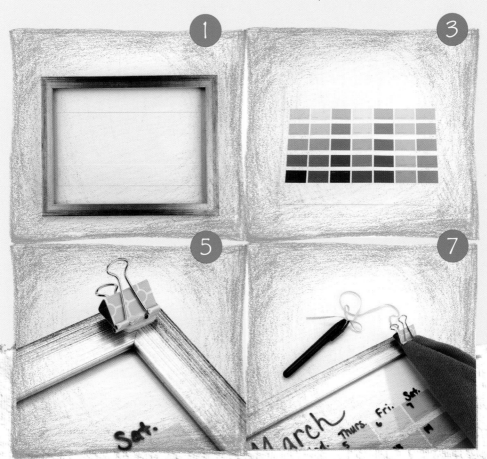

CRAFTING TIPS:

Use a small hole punch on each paint chip before gluing. You can use the punched out shapes as spaces for the month's name.

Be sure to use a frame with glass, not plastic. The marker might not erase completely from plastic.

Check discount or bargain stores for the best deals on microfiber pads and dry erase markers.

Happy Birthday!

This light and fluffy birthday cake-scented soap is like a party in a jar. Just a small scoop will remind the birthday girl or guy that it's a special day.

What You'll Need:

cheese grater

1 bar of soap

4 cups (960 milliliters) water

1 teaspoon (5 mL) glycerin

1 ½ cups (360 mL) solid vegetable shortening

1 cup (240 mL) coconut oil

¼ cup (175 mL) olive oil

birthday cake-scented fragrance oil

jars with lids

sprinkles

1. Grate the bar of soap.
2. Place soap and water in a pot. Gently warm over low to medium heat until most of the soap has dissolved.
3. Remove from heat and add glycerin. Set aside to cool.
4. In a large mixing bowl, combine vegetable shortening and coconut oil. Use an electric mixer until the oils are thick and fluffy like whipped cream.
5. Slowly pour in the olive oil and cooled soap and water mixture. Mix until everything is combined and fluffy.
6. Use a spatula to fold in the fragrance oil. Scoop soap into jars and top with sprinkes.

CRAFTING TIPS:

GLYCERIN CAN BE FOUND AT CRAFT STORES AND PHARMACIES.

TO MAKE A SUGAR SCRUB, ADD 1/3 TO 1/4 CUP (80 TO 120 ML) WHITE OR RAW SUGAR DURING STEP 5.

FOR A CHOCOLATE SCRUB, ADD 2 TO 3 TABLESPOONS (15 TO 30 ML) OF COCOA POWDER.

Say It Out Loud

Words are the ultimate way to express yourself. February is the month of love, but choose words year-round that describe your feelings, words that describe your recipient, or words to inspire.

What You'll Need:
pliers

craft wire

necklace chain

jump rings

16

1. Sketch the word you want to spell. Use cursive script so all the letters flow as one connected line.
2. Use the pliers to make a small, closed loop at the end of the wire.
3. Bend the wire around the words, using your fingers to make the larger curves and the pliers to form detailed twists and bends.
4. Use pliers to tighten the letters until they are shaped to your liking.
5. Trim the wire with a 0.25-inch (0.6-cm)-long tail. Use the pliers to make a closed loop at the end of the word.
6. Attach jump rings to the loop at the beginning and end of the word. Attach the necklace chain to the rings.

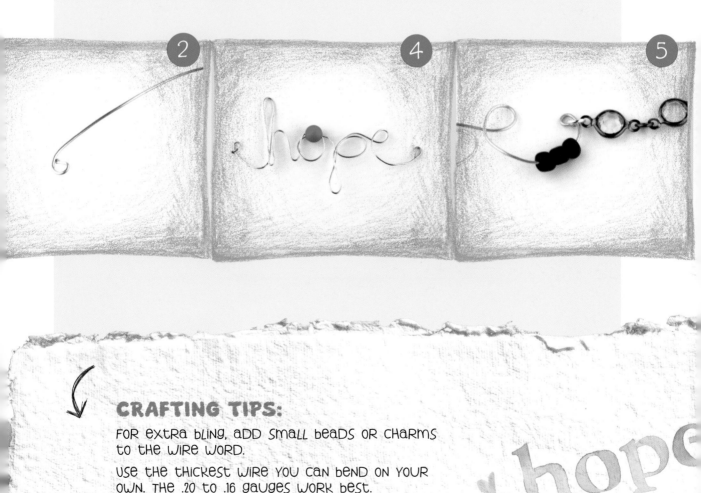

CRAFTING TIPS:

FOR EXTRA BLING, ADD SMALL BEADS OR CHARMS TO THE WIRE WORD.

USE THE THICKEST WIRE YOU CAN BEND ON YOUR OWN. THE .20 TO .16 GAUGES WORK BEST.

Pi Day is Delicious!

Celebrate Pi Day the best way possible—with pie! These handheld snacks are small enough that you can eat 3.14 of them without a second thought.

What You'll Need:

refrigerated pie crust

large cookie cutters

small cookie cutters

your favorite jam or pie filling

egg, beaten

sugar

1. Unroll your pie crust onto a lightly floured work surface. Cut out shapes using large cookie cutters.
2. Pair shapes together so you have a top and bottom. Use the small cookie cutters on the top pieces. This will help vent the filling as the pies bake and prevent overflow
3. Place about 1 tablespoon (15 mL) of jam or filling into the centers of each of the bottoms.
4. Lightly brush the edges of a bottom crust with egg. Place a top crust over the bottom, and use a fork to press the two pieces together.
5. Place pies on a parchment-lined baking sheet. Brush the tops with egg and sprinkle with sugar.
6. Bake at 375 degrees Fahrenheit (190 degrees Celsius) for 10 to 15 minutes or until pies are golden brown. Let cool completely before storing at room temperature.

CRAFTING TIP:

FOR A PRETTY PRESENTATION, WRAP HAND PIES IN PAPER. YOU'LL NEED A PIECE OF SCRAPBOOKING, PARCHMENT, OR TISSUE PAPER LONG ENOUGH TO WRAP AROUND THE PIE. YOU'LL ALSO NEED A PIECE OF WAX PAPER THE SAME SIZE OR SLIGHTLY WIDER. SET THE WAX PAPER ON TOP OF THE DECORATIVE PAPER. THEN PLACE THE PIE FACE DOWN IN THE CENTER. USE A SMALL PIECE OF TAPE TO SEAL THE EDGES OF THE PAPER. THEN FLIP OVER AND TIE A PIECE OF STRING OR RIBBON AROUND THE PIE FOR EXTRA SECURITY.

Plantable Labels

These plantable labels will remind your recipients to "forget-me-not" long after the gift is given. Use these bits of plantable paper as gift tags, greeting card decorations, ornaments, or favors. Tear into small pieces to use for confetti or to cushion delicate wrapped gifts.

What You'll Need:

old paper torn into nickel-sized pieces, enough to make 1 cup (240 mL)

9 by 13 inch (23 by 33 centimeter) pan

1 tablespoon (15 mL) white glue

small seeds

large piece of stiff screen

cooling rack

cookie cutters

1. Place paper and 4 cups (960 mL) of hot water in a blender. Let soak for five minutes.
2. With an adult's help, blend in short bursts on medium-high for 30 to 60 seconds.
3. Drain as much water as you can. Add white glue and seeds.
4. Place screen onto a cooling rack. Make sure there are paper towels or newspaper under the rack, to catch excess water.
5. Press the paper pulp into the cookie cutter shapes. Push hard to make sure the paper pulp is spread evenly. Once the shape is formed, gently remove the cookie cutters. Repeat until all the pulp is used up.
6. Allow paper shapes to dry on the screen for at least 24 hours.

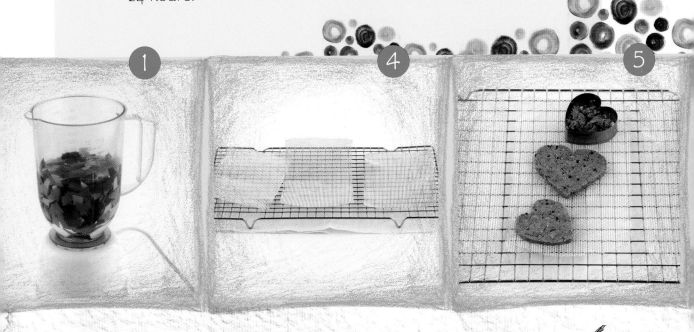

CRAFTING TIPS:

SOME SUGGESTED FLOWERS TO USE: COSMOS, ZINNIAS, MARIGOLDS, FORGET-ME-NOTS, DAISIES, SUNFLOWERS, AND SNAPDRAGONS. USE BOTH ANNUALS AND PERENNIALS FOR YEAR-ROUND BLOOMS.

SOME SUGGESTED HERBS TO USE: BASIL, CHIVES, DILL, THYME, LAVENDER, CILANTRO, SAGE, OREGANO, AND PARSLEY.

SOME SUGGESTED FRUITS AND VEGETABLES: ONIONS, TOMATOES, WATERMELON, CARROTS, STRAWBERRIES, LETTUCE, RADISHES, AND PEPPERS.

Spring Fever

Nice weather means more outside time. Make it easy for your friends and family to dress up their outdoor areas with some bright springtime patio pillows.

What You'll Need:

seam ripper

placemat with both a front and back piece

seam ripper

plastic grocery bag

polyester fiberfill

stapler

needle and thread

outdoor waterproofing spray

1. Locate the edge on the placemat where the front and back are sewn together. Most of the seams will be hidden, but there should be a small area where the stitches show. Use the seam ripper to open the seams there.
2. Push the grocery bag into the placemat.
3. Stuff the placemat with the polyester fiberfill. Make sure the fiberfill goes into the bag, not between the bag and the placemat.
4. Roll the opening of the plastic bag up, as tight as you can. Use the stapler to seal the bag shut. Stuff the bag into the placemat.
5. Sew the placemat shut. (See sewing instructions on page 23 for tips.)
6. Coat the pillow thoroughly with waterproofing spray. Pay special attention to the seams.

CRAFTING TIP:

WRAP YOUR PILLOWS UP IN AN OUTDOOR BLANKET OR PRESENT THEM IN A BASKET OR LARGE FLOWER POT ALONG WITH OTHER OUTDOOR ESSENTIALS, SUCH AS BUG SPRAY AND CITRONELLA CANDLES.

Mother's Day Bouquet

Flowers and chocolates are what you get your mom when you're out of ideas. Update the cliché Mom's Day gift and make her this edible bouquet.

What You'll Need:

floral foam

light green tissue paper

wicker basket

skewers

green cupcake liners

unfrosted chocolate cupcakes

buttercream frosting

For the Frosting:

½ cup (120 mL) unsalted butter, softened

½ teaspoon (2.5 mL) vanilla extract

2 cups (480 mL) powdered sugar

1–2 tablespoons (15 to 30 mL) milk

food coloring (optional)

1. Wrap floral foam with tissue paper and place in the basket. Press skewers in the foam anywhere you want a cupcake.
2. Place each cupcake inside a green liner. This will make your bouquet look more like flowers.
3. Press the bottoms of the cupcakes into the tip skewers. Fold and tuck tissue paper between the cupcakes to make the bouquet look more full.
4. To make the frosting, place the butter and vanilla in a large bowl. Use a hand mixer to whip them together until light and fluffy. Alternate adding sugar and milk until the ingredients are mixed well. Scrape the sides of the bowl with a spatula often to make sure everything is incorporated.
5. Add food coloring, if desired. The frosting should be thick, creamy, and spreadable.

Piping Flowers:

For the pink rose: Put a #81 tip on a piping bag and fill bag with frosting. Hold the bag with the rounded tip facing down, like a smile. Gently squeeze the frosting bag to create a cone in the center of the cupcake. Pipe a third of the way around the cone to make a petal. Overlap the tip slightly with the last petal and pipe a second petal. Continue until the entire cupcake is covered.

For the purple mum: Put a #81 tip on a piping bag. Hold the bag at a 45-degree angle, with the rounded tip facing down. Squeeze the bag firmly to create a 1/2-inch (1.2-cm) long petal. Lift the tip slightly to release the petal. Continue creating petals around the entire cupcake.

25

Graduation Lei

School graduates in Hawaii are given leis to celebrate. Leis made of flowers or kukui nuts are traditional, but candy leis are much more fun!

What You'll Need:

4 foot by 1 foot (1.2 by 0.3 meter) piece of plastic knitted mesh

candy

ribbon

For the flower:

a dollar bill

tape

craft wire

1. Knot one end of the mesh. Place a piece of candy in the center of the mesh, near the knot.
2. Twist the mesh so the candy is trapped inside. Tie a knot at the base of the candy to hold it in place.
3. Repeat placing candy, twisting, and tying until the lei is complete.
4. Tie the ends of the mesh together to make a necklace.

For the flower:

1. Fold the dollar bill accordion-style.
2. Fold the accordion in half.
3. Find the ends of one side and tape together. Repeat for the other end.
4. Thread craft wire near the centers of the taped ends.
5. Re-fold any edges that may have rumpled while taping.
6. Attach the flower to your lei with the craft wire.

CRAFTING TIPS:

OTHER ITEMS, SUCH AS PLASTIC JEWELRY OR SMALL CHANGE, CAN BE USED IN PLACE OF CANDY.

IF YOU CAN'T FIND MESH, YOU CAN USE PLASTIC WRAP OR EVEN FABRIC.

Coozie and Cool

Whether you're at a game, practice, rehearsal, or just at home watching TV, it's important to keep your beverages cool.

What You'll Need:

newspaper

ruler

compass

chalk

thin neoprene

8 x 12 inch (20 x 30 cm) piece of fabric

1. Create a template using the newspaper, ruler, and compass. Draw two 4-inch (10 cm) squares with a 2 inch (5 cm) circle in the center. Cut the template out.
2. Use chalk to trace template onto the uncolored side of the neoprene. Cut out the template.
3. Fold the neoprene in half with the patterned sides facing in.
4. Sew up the square sides of the coozie. Then turn the coozie right-side-out.
5. Fold the fabric into thirds.
6. Sew along the fold lines. Then sew the short ends together.
7. Slip the fabric over the neoprene. Use a few loose stitches to attach the fabric.

Sewing by Hand:

Slide the thread through the eye of the needle. Tie the end of the thread into a knot. Poke the needle through the underside of the fabric. Pull the thread through the fabric to knotted end. Poke your needle back through the fabric and up again to make a stitch.

Continue weaving the needle in and out of the fabric, making small stitches in a straight line. When you are finished sewing, make a loose stitch. Thread the needle through the loop and pull tight. Cut off remaining thread.

CRAFTING TIP:

IF YOU CAN'T FIND NEOPRENE AT YOUR LOCAL FABRIC STORE, LOOK AROUND ONLINE. YOU'LL FIND MORE COLOR AND PRINT CHOICES ONLINE TOO.

First Day of Summer

School's out, the sun is shining—what better way to spend the day than at the pool? Fold the towel out for sunbathing, or flip over and fold up to carry beach or yoga mats.

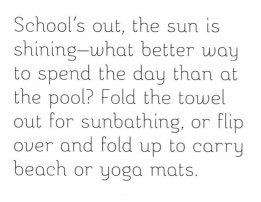

What You'll Need:

beach towel

needle and thread

two 30-inch (76-cm) pieces of ribbon

pins

1. Place your towel on your work surface. The fluffy side should be facing up. Fold the short edges in about 6 inches (15 cm) on each side.
2. Fold the towel in half, so the folded edges touch. These edges will be the top of your bag.
3. Decide where you want your handles. Pin the ribbon handles to the bag. Unfold the edges of the towel. Sew the ends of the handles onto the bag.
4. Cut the hand towel in half. This will be the bag's pocket. Place half of the hand towel in the center of the bag. The hemmed edge of the hand towel should be just an inch or two below the handles.
5. Open the hand towel like a book, with the cut end as the center. Sew the cut end to the bag. Then flip the hand towel back over, and sew up the sides to finish the pocket.
6. Repeat steps 4-5 on the other side of the bag.

CRAFTING AND GIFTING TIPS:

Leave the sides of the bag unstitched so it can be unfolded and used as a beach towel.

Fill your beach bag's pockets with suntan lotion, flip flops, sunglasses, water balloons, reusable tumblers, and other summer essentials.

Fall Hanger

Colorful felt is an easy way to update an old wreath. Choose fall colors, or use any variety of shades that look nice together. This wreath is a nice holiday or hostess gift.

What You'll Need:

scissors

5-inch (13-cm) long piece of cardboard

pen

9 by 12 inch (23 by 33 cm) sheets of felt in different colors

foam wreath

hot glue gun and glue

ribbon

floral embellishment

1. Cut a scalloped template out of the cardboard. The scallops should be about 2 inches (5 cm) at the widest points.
2. Snip each piece of felt in half. Lay the template over a piece of felt. Use the pen to trace the template onto the felt. Repeat until there is no more room. Then cut out the template shapes.
3. Repeat step 2 with the remaining felt pieces.
4. Wrap a piece of felt around the top of the foam wreath. Glue in place.
5. Wrap and glue another piece of felt around the wreath. Overlap the first piece slightly.
6. Continue wrapping and gluing until the entire wreath is covered.
7. Use hot glue to attach floral embellishment to your wreath. Use more ribbon to hang the wreath.

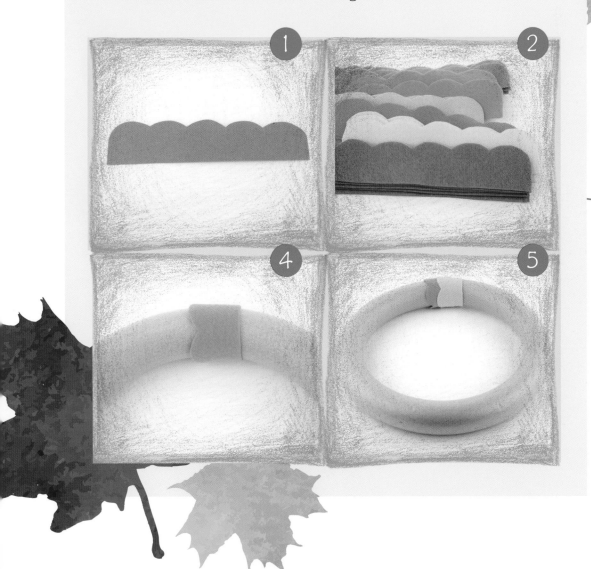

Edible Ornaments

You won't have to worry about these ornaments breaking or being lost. These festive treats will decorate your host's house—that is, until they've all been eaten!

What You'll Need:

1 9 x 13 inch cake or 2 9-inch round cakes, any flavor

1 tub of frosting, any flavor

candy melts, any color

soft paintbrush

silver luster dust

white candy melts

fruit roll-up

mini chocolate candy cups (such as mini Reese's or Rolos)

1. Crumble the cake into a bowl so there are no large pieces.
2. Add a spoonful of frosting to the crumbled cake. Continue adding spoonfuls of frosting and mixing until the mixture is a moist dough that you can mold into balls. You'll probably use most of a tub of frosting.
3. Cover a baking sheet with wax paper. Roll the cake dough into 2-inch (5 cm) balls. Arrange on the baking sheet.
4. Melt a small amount of melting wafers according to package directions. Melt just one color at a time.
5. Use a toothpick or skewer to dip a cake ball into the melted candy. Let excess candy drip off. Then place ball on top of an unmelted candy melt. This will hide any flaws and give your cake ball stability. Continue until all cake balls are dipped. Let the candy dry for at least 30 minutes.

6. To give your ornaments some shine, use a paintbrush and lightly brush luster dust over a cake ball.

7. Place the white candy melts in a small zip-top bag. Leave the bag open and microwave on the defrost setting for 30 seconds. Squeeze the melted candy to one corner. If the wafers are not soft yet, microwave on defrost 30 seconds more. With a kitchen shears, snip off the corner of the bag.

8. Use the melted candy to decorate the cake balls. Swirls, trees, snowflakes, stripes, and dots are just a few ideas. Let dry for at least one hour.

9. With an adult's help, cut the fruit roll-up into very thin strips. Trim down to shorter pieces, to make hangers for your ornaments. Use melted candy melts to connect a hanger to a mini chocolate candy cup.

10. In a small dish, combine a small amount of luster dust with an equal amount of clear alcohol. Use a paintbrush to color the mini chocolate candy cups.

11. Use more melted candy melts to glue the mini chocolate candy cups to the cake balls.

12. Use more luster dust to paint the piped designs from step 8, if desired.

Try these other decorating ideas!

- Use disco dust, a nontoxic glitter, instead of luster dust. Brush cake balls with a moistened paintbrush. Then dip your brush into disco dust and paint onto the cake balls. Once the disco dust has dried completely, use a dry brush to remove any excess.

- Use sprinkles or nonpareils to decorate ornaments.

- Set cake balls in paper candy cups or tissue paper. Then wrap in a festive container or vintage ornament box.

- Sprinkle fine sanding sugar or edible glitter over your piped designs while the melted candy is still wet.

Eco Gifts

Upcycled Gifts You Can Make

Show your recipient you value their friendship while valuing the Earth at the same time. Reuse and refill treasured objects with great new gifts that keep on giving.

40   PRETTY PIN-UP

42   FANCY FLOWERS

Pretty Pin-Up

This fabric-covered corkboard can be used for a bulletin or organizer board, a jewelry hanger, a set of coasters, or even a small piece of art. Because cork is a sustainable product, it's a great eco gift.

What You'll Need:

iron

three 8-inch (20 cm) squares of fabric

7-inch (18 centimeter) round corkboard

hot glue

ribbon

push pins

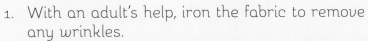

1. With an adult's help, iron the fabric to remove any wrinkles.
2. Lay one piece of fabric flat, pattern-side-down. Center the cork on the fabric. Glue the fabric onto the corkboard. Cut off any excess fabric and use glue to tidy up any overlaps.
3. Fold a second square of fabric in half. Iron the fold to make a crisp seam.
4. Lay the folded fabric over half the cork to make a pocket. Glue the fabric to the back of the corkboard. Trim any excess fabric.
5. Repeat step 3 with the third fabric square.
6. Set the folded fabric over a third of the cork to make a pocket. Glue the fabric to the back of the corkboard. Trim any excess fabric and let dry completely.
7. Use glue to add a ribbon loop to the back of the corkboard for easy hanging.
8. Press pins into the corkboard to decorate.

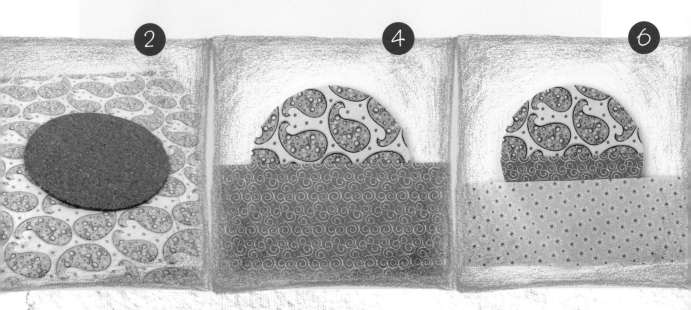

CRAFTING TIPS:

MAKE ONE BIG CORKBOARD OR CREATE SEVERAL SMALLER BOARDS COVERED WITH COORDINATING FABRICS.

DECORATE LARGE FLAT-BACKED TACKS WITH MATCHING FABRIC. TRIM FABRIC PIECES TO THE SAME SIZE OF THE TACK HEADS, AND ATTACH WITH A THIN LAYER OF DECOUPAGE GLUE. ADD A LAYER OF DECOUPAGE GLUE OVER THE TOP OF THE FABRIC TO SEAL.

USE A SINGLE LAYER OF FABRIC TO COVER THE BOARD AND OMIT THE RIBBON FOR A PRETTY TABLE TRIVET.

Fancy Flowers

You've got the gift wrap, but no present! What to do? There's no need to worry when you've got a beautiful bouquet at your fingertips.

What You'll Need:

one 8-10 sheet package of tissue paper

3.5 inch (9 cm) scalloped paper punch

stapler

markers

floral stems and tape

1.5 inch (3.8 cm) wide satin ribbon

corsage pins

1. Unfold the tissue paper. Use the paper punch to cut out a stack of circles and staple each stack in the center.
2. Use markers to color the outer edges of the paper stack, if desired.
3. Begin fluffing the top layer of paper toward the center. Continue until all layers except the bottom layer are fluffed.
4. Fold the bottom layer of tissue paper over a wire stem. Wrap floral tape tightly around the paper and stem.
5. Repeat steps 1–4 until you have enough flowers to make a bouquet.
6. Gather flowers into a bouquet. Wrap the stems tightly with ribbon.
7. For a fancier stem treatment, wrap the ribbon all the way to the bottom of the stems and then back up to the top. Keep the ribbon as flat as possible.
8. Secure the ribbon with corsage pins. Pins should be placed at a downward angle and in a straight line down the entire ribbon wrap.

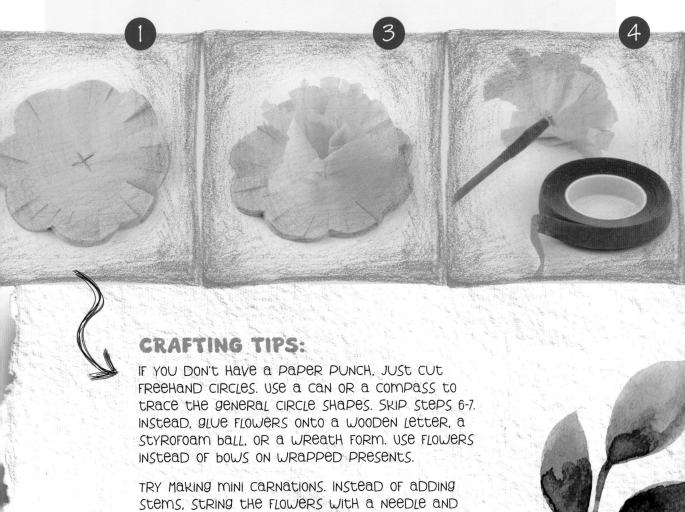

CRAFTING TIPS:

IF YOU DON'T HAVE A PAPER PUNCH, JUST CUT FREEHAND CIRCLES. USE A CAN OR A COMPASS TO TRACE THE GENERAL CIRCLE SHAPES. SKIP STEPS 6-7. INSTEAD, GLUE FLOWERS ONTO A WOODEN LETTER, A STYROFOAM BALL, OR A WREATH FORM. USE FLOWERS INSTEAD OF BOWS ON WRAPPED PRESENTS.

TRY MAKING MINI CARNATIONS. INSTEAD OF ADDING STEMS, STRING THE FLOWERS WITH A NEEDLE AND THREAD TO MAKE A GARLAND.

Labels and Lids

There are many recipes for gifts in a jar. But there's no rule saying the jar can't be as great as the gift that's inside!

What You'll Need:

jar with lid

decorative paper

decoupage glue and paintbrush

masking or painters tape

chalkboard paint and paintbrush

craft knife

CRAFTING TIP:
IF YOUR JAR HAS A TWO-PIECE LID, USE SUPERGLUE TO CONNECT THE LID TO THE RING. LET DRY COMPLETELY BEFORE CONTINUING.

1. Trace the lid onto the plain side of the decorative paper.
2. Cut a circle at least ¼ inch (0.6 cm) larger around than the lid. Snip thin strips all the way around the circle, from the edge of the paper to the edge of your traced circle.
3. Paint a thin layer of decoupage glue onto the top of the lid. Gently press the paper onto the lid, smoothing out any bubbles.
4. Paint a thin layer of decoupage glue onto the inside of the lid. Fold and press the strips along the circle's edge into the glue. Let dry completely. Add another layer of glue over the entire paper-covered area. Let dry completely.
5. Tape off the area of the jar you want to paint. Apply a thin coat of chalkboard paint. Let dry at least 30 minutes. Add additional coats if desired.
6. Remove tape. With an adult's help, use a craft knife to remove any areas where the paint may have scuffed or bled through the tape. Allow paint to cure for at least three days before using for writing.

Here are a few ideas on filling your gift jar:

- cookies, candy, or other sweet selections
- pampering items such as nail polish, lip gloss, and sample-sized sugar scrubs, body butters, and bath bombs
- mixes for treats such as soups, dips, baked goods, or drinks
- a sewing kit with a simple pattern, fabric to make the pattern, and thread, needles, buttons, and pins

Puny Plastic

Reuse those plastic containers instead of tossing them! Turn big, bulky pieces of trash into shrunken bits of beauty.

What You'll Need:

measuring tape

clean plastic container

sandpaper

stamp and stamp pad

thin-tipped permanent markers

cookie sheet lined with parchment paper or tinfoil

thin glove or oven mitt

object about the same size as your finger, such as a dowel, marker, spoon handle, nail polish bottle handle, etc.

clear nail polish

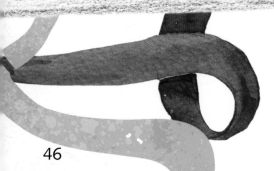

1. Use the measuring tape to estimate your ring's finished length and width. Multiply both measurements by 10.
2. Cut a piece from the plastic container that matches your multiplied measurements. Use scissors to round off the corners.
3. Sand one side of the plastic until the surface is rough. Smooth the sharp corners of the plastic with sandpaper.
4. Decorate the sanded side of the plastic with stamps and markers. Colors will concentrate after shrinking, so keep things simple to avoid muddy hues.

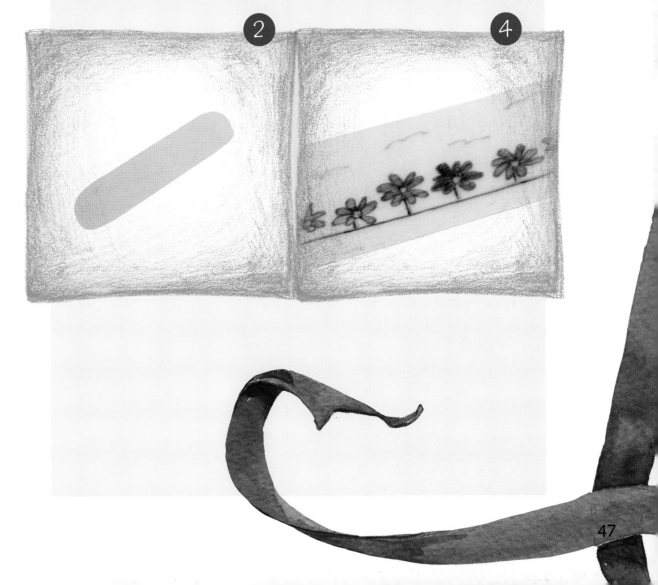

5. Place plastic on cookie sheet. Have an adult place sheet in a 350 degree Fahrenheit (180 degree Celsius) oven for a few minutes. The plastic will curl and then uncurl. When it's flat again, it's ready to come out.

6. Put on the glove or oven mitt to protect your hand. Remove cookie sheet from oven. Working quickly, wrap the plastic strip around the object the same size as your finger. Hold the plastic until it has cooled.

7. Once your ring has cooled completely, coat with a thin layer of clear nail polish to protect your design.

CRAFTING TIPS:

USE #6 PLASTIC FOR THIS PROJECT. THE PLASTIC NUMBER CAN USUALLY BE FOUND ON THE BOTTOM OF THE CONTAINER. LOOK FOR CLEAR PLASTIC CLAMSHELL CONTAINERS. USUALLY BAKED GOODS, BERRIES, AND TAKE-OUT MEALS ARE SOLD IN THIS TYPE OF CONTAINER.

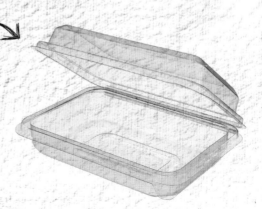

MORE CRAFTING TIPS:

Your plastic may shrink more less than 10 times its size. Some plastics may shrink as little as 3 times their length. Others may shrink more than the 10 times written here. Experiment with different starting lengths of plastic to get the right size ring.

If you don't shape your ring fast enough and it doesn't look just right, don't worry! Have an adult pop it back in the oven with the ring tips in the air. Reheat for about 30 seconds—it should re-flatten. Then try to shape into a ring again.

To give your ring extra dimension, make and shrink flowers or other decorations and glue them onto the ring. But don't stop there—make matching bracelets and necklaces too! Cut the plastic into shapes, and then use a hole punch to make holes before baking. Use jump rings to make a bracelet, or thread onto a chain for a necklace. For a cuff bracelet, follow the ring instructions but start with a much larger piece of plastic. You can find 8 x 10 inch (20.3 x 25.4 cm) sheets online or in craft stores.

Colorful Charge

With a few simple steps, you can create a cute charging station that keeps your electronics in one place and cords tucked safely out of the way.

What You'll Need:

empty soap or shampoo bottle

craft knife

sandpaper

decoupage glue and foam brush

fabric

washi tape

Velcro dots

GIFTING TIP:

FILL THE CHARGING STATION WITH INEXPENSIVE CHARGING CORDS, CELL PHONE COVERS OR SKINS, DUST PLUGS, STYLUSES, EAR BUDS, AND OTHER SMALL ACCESSORIES.

1. Starting at the top of the bottle, cut halfway down the sides. Cut off the front half of the bottle to make a pocket.
2. Trim a square the size of an outlet plug in the back of the bottle.
3. Once you're satisfied with your cuts, sand down all edges until they are even and no longer sharp. Also lightly sandpaper the inside and outside of the bottle.
4. Brush a light coat of decoupage glue onto the outside of the bottle. Press fabric into the glue, wrapping and pressing fabric to avoid bunching and bubbles.
5. Trim any excess fabric. Then add a layer of decoupage glue over everything. Let dry completely.
6. Measure a piece of washi tape 7 inches (20.3 cm) long. Fold the tape in half, sticky sides together. Leave a 0.5 inch (1.3 cm) length from the end unstuck.
7. Flip the tape over and press the sticky end of the tape inside front pocket. The rest of the tape should hang out the front of the bottle.
8. Attach the Velcro to the tape at the top of the front pocket. Stick the other piece of Velcro on the reverse end of the tape. This will create a loop to hold headphones or any excess charge cord.

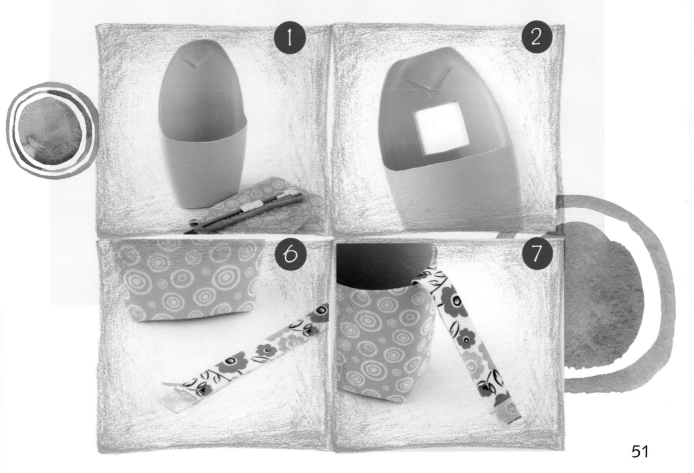

Solid Scents

Solid perfumes are the perfect pocket-sized gift. They can be customized to match your recipient's favorite scents. You can go all natural by using essential oil, or buy fragrance oil. You can also use your favorite bottled perfume.

What You'll Need:

1 tablespoon (15 mL) beeswax

1 tablespoon olive oil

scent, such as essential oil, fragrance oil, or your favorite perfume

old containers, such as lip balm tubes, bottle caps, makeup compacts, or lockets

1. If using solid beeswax instead of pellets, grate or chop until the beeswax is in small pieces.
2. Place beeswax and olive oil in a microwave-safe container. Heat for 15 seconds. Then remove from the microwave and stir. Continue heating and stirring until the beeswax is completely melted.
3. Quickly stir in scent. Add until the mixture smells as strong as you'd like. This could be between 20 and 40 drops of essential oil.
4. Pour the mixture into your containers. Let set until solid, between 15 and 30 minutes.

CRAFTING TIPS:

YOU CAN MAKE THIS RECIPE IN ANY QUANTITY. JUST BE SURE TO USE ONE PART BEESWAX TO ONE PART OLIVE OIL.

TO TURN THIS RECIPE INTO A LOTION BAR, ADD ONE PART COCONUT OIL TO THE RECIPE. USE LARGER CONTAINERS, SUCH AS DEODORANT TUBES, PUSH POP CONTAINERS, OR MINT TINS, OR POUR INTO MUFFIN TINS OR SOAP MOLDS.

TO TURN THIS RECIPE INTO LIP BALM, ADD A SQUEEZE OF HONEY. STIR IN A BIT OF LIPSTICK OR EDIBLE GLITTER FOR COLOR, OR A LITTLE POWDERED DRINK MIX FOR COLOR AND FLAVOR. (SKIP THE ESSENTIAL OILS IF YOU USE THE POWDER.)

SOME SUGGESTED ESSENTIAL OILS INCLUDE MINT, CITRUSES SUCH AS LEMON OR ORANGE, LAVENDER, TEA TREE, ROSE, AND VANILLA. TRY COMBINING SCENTS—LEMON AND MINT OR ORANGE AND VANILLA ARE TWO GOOD CHOICES.

Infinity Tee

Nothing says "eco gift" like recycling a well-loved tee. Use a favorite shirt or just pick something in your recipient's color scheme.

What You'll Need:

2 soft T-shirts in different colors: XL or XXL work best

fabric scissors

measuring tape

needle and thread

1. Lay a shirt flat on your work surface. Cut straight across the shirt from armpit to armpit. Discard the top part.
2. Measure 15 inches (38 cm) down from your cut line. Cut straight across. You should have a wide loop of fabric.
3. Fold the loop lengthwise so the cut ends are together. Sew down the whole cut side. Then turn inside out, so your stitches are on the inside.
4. Repeat steps 1-3 with the second shirt.
5. Fold one fabric strip in half and lay flat on your work surface, with the ends facing out. Fold the other fabric strip in half, and face it the opposite direction. Its looped end should overlap the first fabric strip.
6. Slide your hand through the fabric loop on the bottom. Gently pull the ends of the other fabric strip through. You should have a donut-shaped knot.
7. Repeat step 6 as many times as desired. Gently pull the knot tight each time. This should give you a braid with overlapping color layers.
8. Sew the ends of the scarf together.

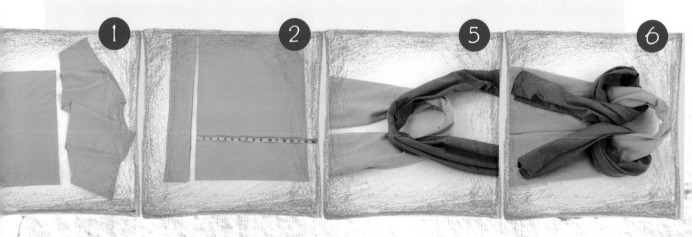

Sewing by Hand:

Slide the thread through the eye of the needle. Tie the end of the thread into a knot. Poke the needle through the underside of the fabric. Pull the thread through the fabric to knotted end. Poke your needle back through the fabric and up again to make a stitch.

Continue weaving the needle in and out of the fabric, making small stitches in a straight line. When you are finished sewing, make a loose stitch. Thread the needle through the loop and pull tight. Cut off remaining thread.

Canine Carry-All

Dog food bags come in a variety of colors and styles. And because they're meant to hold lots of heavy kibble, they can take everyday wear and tear. Upcycle to make the ultimate tote for the dog lover in your life.

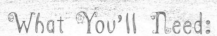

What You'll Need:

scissors

clean 30 pound (13.6 kilogram) dog food bag

measuring tape

newspaper

duct tape

clear packing tape

towel

iron

1. Cut along the long side and the bottom of the bag. Open the bag and lay it flat on your work surface.
2. Trim two long strips from the bag, about 20 inches (51 cm) long and 0.75 inch (2 cm) wide. Set the long strips aside to use for handles.
3. Measure and cut out a pattern from the newspaper. The pattern should be 19.5 inches (50 cm) wide and 17.5 inches (44.5 cm) tall. Cut out a 3 inch (7.6 cm) square from the two bottom corners.
4. Trace the pattern onto the dog food bag. Then cut out the pieces. You should have enough space to cut out two pattern pieces.
5. Lay both of the food bag pieces out flat, with the plain sides facing up. Overlap the tabbed edges. This will be the bottom of the bag.
6. Duct tape the tabbed edges together on the inside of the bag. Turn over, and use clear tape on the outside seams.

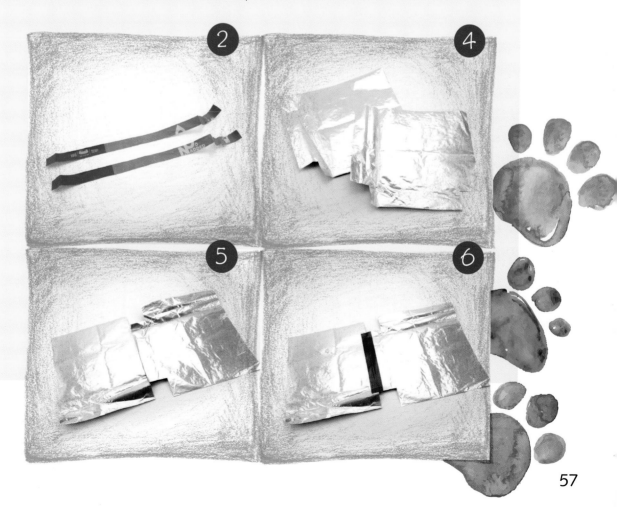

7. Fold the edges together to make the sides of the bag. Repeat step 5, using duct tape on the inside of the bag and clear tape on the outside.

8. Place a towel over the folded edges. With an adult's help, use an iron on low heat over the folds. This will give you nice, crisp creases. The towel will prevent the iron from melting or burning the bag.

9. Once the sides are complete, make a cut about 2 inches (5 cm) long at the top of each corner of the bag. Fold the edges into the bag. Iron the folds, then secure with duct tape.

10. Measure a piece of clear tape, about 21 inches (53 cm) long. Lay it sticky-side-up on your work surface. Center one of the handles you cut in step 2 over the tape. Fold the excess tape over the handle. Repeat so you have two handles.

11. Decide where you want to place the handles. Attach one handle to the bag, leaving the bottom inch (2.5 cm) of both ends uncovered.

12. Fold the bottoms of the handle up over the duct tape. Use more duct tape to press the bottoms to the bag. This will give your handle more stability.

13. Repeat with the second handle.

CRAFTING TIPS:

TO GET RID OF THE DOG FOOD SMELL, RINSE THE BAG WELL WITH DISH SOAP AND LET AIR DRY OVERNIGHT.

DON'T FEEL LIMITED TO DOG, CAT, RABBIT, LIVESTOCK, AND HORSE FEED BAGS ARE OTHER GREAT CHOICES. CAT LITTER, BIRD SEED, AND BULK RICE BAGS WORK WELL TOO.

ASK AROUND TO SEE IF ANYONE HAS BAGS THAT MIGHT WORK BEFORE YOU BUY. IF YOU DO BUY THE BAG BUT DON'T NEED WHAT'S INSIDE, CONSIDER DONATING TO AN ANIMAL RESCUE OR FOOD SHELF.

Books 'n Birds

Treasured tales get a new life
with this page-turning birdhouse.
Bring a little of your library
outdoors with a plain birdhouse
and some glue.

What You'll Need:

cardboard

wooden birdhouse

craft knife

hardcover picture book

outdoor decoupage glue and foam brush

1. Make a cardboard template of the front, sides, and back of the birdhouse. Be sure to trace over the entrance hole and perch.
2. Have an adult cut all the pages from the book with a craft knife. Choose which pages you want to use to decorate the birdhouse.
3. Lay the templates over your chosen pages. Trim to fit.
4. Brush a thin layer of decoupage glue over the front of the birdhouse. Carefully press your trimmed book page into the glue. Cover with more decoupage.
5. Repeat with the rest of the birdhouse until all sides are covered.
6. Brush a thin layer of decoupage over the roof of the birdhouse. Set the book cover over the top. Brush the top, sides, and underside of the book thoroughly with decoupage. Let the entire birdhouse dry completely.
7. Add two to three more layers of decoupage, letting each layer dry before adding the next.

CRAFTING TIPS:

IF YOU CAN'T FIND OUTDOOR DECOUPAGE GLUE, USE REGULAR DECOUPAGE GLUE. THEN ADD TWO OR THREE COATS OF A SPRAY SEALANT.

IF YOUR BOOK COVER IS TOO LARGE FOR THE BIRDHOUSE ROOF, TRIM IT INTO STRIPS OR TILES AND OVERLAP THEM LIKE SHINGLES. USE WOOD GLUE TO MAKE SURE THEY STAY ON.

Special Salt Dough

Salt dough is an all-natural, chemical-free way to show you care. Toss a few everyday ingredients together, decorate, and gift! Ornaments, gift tags, and place settings are only a few salt dough ideas.

What You'll Need:

2 cups (480 mL) flour

1 cup (240 mL) salt

1 cup water

rolling pin

parchment paper

large cookie cutter

small cookie cutter

letter stamps and stamp pad

patterned stamps

sandpaper

1. In a large bowl, mix flour and salt. Add water and mix with your hands until the mixture is doughlike.
2. Roll dough out on parchment paper to 0.25 inch (0.6 cm) thick.
3. Use the large cookie cutter to cut out tags.
4. Punch out shapes from the center of each tag with the small cookie cutter.
5. Use letter stamps coated with ink to press your message into the tags. Use patterned stamps for more decoration.
6. Set tags onto a baking sheet lined with parchment paper. With an adult's supervision, bake at 250 degrees F (120 degrees C) for at least 2 hours, or until tags are dry but not browned. The tags are done when they sound hollow when tapped.
7. Gently sand edges until smooth.

GIFTING TIPS:

THIS SALT DOUGH CRAFT IS VERSATILE. TRY THESE VARIATIONS:

- FOR COASTERS, USE A DRINKING GLASS TO CUT OUT DOUGH. SPRAY WITH ACRYLIC SEALER AFTER BAKING TO PROTECT YOUR ART.

- FOR KEYCHAINS, PENDANTS, OR ORNAMENTS, MAKE A HOLE IN THE DOUGH WITH A SKEWER BEFORE BAKING.

- TURN INTO MAGNETS BY ATTACHING STICKY-BACK MAGNETS TO EACH TAG.

- USE LEAVES OR SEASHELLS AS NATURAL STAMPS. COLOR THE INDENTATIONS WITH ACRYLIC PAINT.

- FOR MORE COLOR, KNEAD FOOD COLORING INTO THE DOUGH BEFORE ROLLING.

Hidden Treasures

Candles are a tried and true gift, but what's a person to do with the wax leftover at the end? Don't throw away your old jarred candles. Instead, turn them into the gift that keeps on giving. Toss in a tiny trinket for a fun surprise!

What You'll Need:

large slow cooker

jarred candles in at least three colors; make sure the scents are similar

candle wick

clean candle jar

tinfoil

trinket, such as jewelry, heat-safe toys, or charms

fine glitter

1. Pour several inches of warm water into a large slow cooker. Place jarred candles into slow cooker and heat on high for one hour, or until wax is melted.
2. Dip the metal bottom of the candle wick into some melted wax. Press the wick into the clean candle jar.
3. Fold a double layer of tinfoil around your trinket for protection. Make it as small as possible, and seal the edges well.
4. Carefully pour wax from one jarred candle into the clean candle jar. Use tongs or potholders if the jar is hot. Gently press the trinket into the warm wax.
5. Once the wax has hardened, add another layer of melted wax from another jarred candle. Continue layering until your candle is complete and the trinket is completely covered. Sprinkle glitter over the final layer.
6. Trim wick to 0.5 inch (1.3 cm) long.

CRAFTING TIPS:

IF THE JAR YOU WANT TO USE FOR YOUR NEW CANDLE STILL HAS WAX ON THE BOTTOM, THE FIRST STEP IS TO CLEAN IT OUT! WITH AN ADULT'S' HELP, POUR BOILING WATER INTO THE JARRED CANDLE. THIS WILL SOFTEN THE WAX. USE A BUTTER KNIFE TO GENTLY PRY THE WAX LOOSE. ONCE THE WATER HAS COOLED COMPLETELY, REMOVE THE WAX FROM THE JAR. WASH THE JAR IN WARM, SOAPY WATER.

MAKE SURE YOUR CANDLE SCENTS GO TOGETHER! PAIR ALL HOLIDAY SCENTS OR ALL TROPICAL SCENTS. IF YOU DON'T HAVE ENOUGH OLD WAX TO MAKE A NEW CANDLE, USE PURCHASED WAX TO FILL THE CANDLE JAR.

TO REUSE SMALL AMOUNTS OF WAX, POUR INTO SMALL SILICONE MOLDS OR ICE CUBE TRAYS. YOUR RECIPIENT CAN USE THEM IN CANDLE WARMERS.

Silver Suncatchers

Make a garden greener with these recyclable silvery stakes. These glittering decorations are sure to catch the eye.

What You'll Need:

empty soda can

sharp scissors

butterfly paper punch

sandpaper

nail

spray primer paint

colored spray paint

metal garden stake

industrial-strength glue

1. With an adult's help, cut off the top and bottom of the soda can. Then make a cut along the side of the can to make a flat sheet of aluminum.
2. Cut out butterfly shapes with the paper punch. Use sandpaper to smooth any rough edges.
3. Give the butterflies dimension by using the nail to draw textures or fold lines onto the aluminum.
4. In a well-ventilated area, coat the butterflies with a layer of primer. Let dry completely.
5. Coat the butterflies with a layer of spray paint. Let dry completely. Repeat if necessary.
6. Attach a stake to the bottom of a butterfly with a bead of industrial-strength glue.

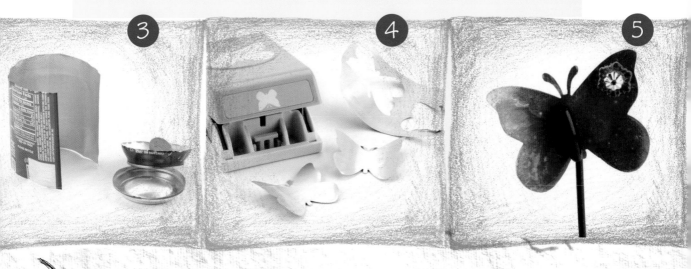

GIFTING TIPS:

YOU CAN USE THESE STAKES OUTDOORS OR AS DECORATIONS IN A BOUQUET OF FLOWERS. BUT THAT'S NOT ALL! TRY ONE OF THESE OTHER IDEAS TOO:

- SKIP THE STAKES AND USE FISHING LINE TO ATTACH THE BUTTERFLIES TO A DOWEL OR METAL CRAFT RING TO MAKE A WIND CHIME OR SUN CATCHER.

- INDIVIDUAL BUTTERFLIES MAKE A PRETTY PACKAGE TOPPER.

- GLUE BUTTERFLIES ONTO A HEADBAND OR RING. ADD TINY BEADS FOR EXTRA DETAIL.

- ATTACH BUTTERFLIES TO A PAPER LANTERN OR OTHER LIGHT COVERING.

In Good Taste

Great Gifts to Make, Eat and Share!

They say the fastest way to a person's heart is through their stomach. Get there even faster with sweet and savory homemade gifts!

70

DELICIOUS DIPS

72

MADE WITH LOAF

76 BARK BITES

88 FRIENDSHIP KETCHUP

78 FRESH FRIDGE PICKLES

90 SPAGHETT-ME-NOT

80 TASTE BOUQUET

92 SWIRLY SWEETS

84 POWDERY PILLOWS

94 JUST BECAUSE

86 GET WELL SOON STEW-N

96 SHARING BASKETS

Delicious Dips

A few simple herbs and spices can create an easy edible gift. With dozens of flavors and tastes to choose from, it's easy to customize these seasoning blends to fit anyone's palate.

Taco Seasoning:

2 tablespoons (30 milliliters) chili powder

1 tablespoon (15 mL) paprika

1 tablespoon cumin

1 teaspoon (5 mL) garlic powder

1 teaspoon onion powder

pinch of Cayenne pepper

Instructions:

Brown 1 pound (455 grams) ground beef. Add entire ornament of seasoning and tablespoon water. Simmer for at least 15 minutes.

Pumpkin Pie Spice:
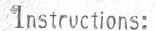

4 tablespoons (60 mL) cinnamon

2 tablespoons (30 mL) ginger

1 tablespoon (15 mL) cloves

1 teaspoon (5 mL) nutmeg

Instructions:

Sprinkle over cocoa, eggnog, or sweet potatoes. Mix with a 15 ounce (415 gram) can of pumpkin, two 3.4 ounce (97 gram) boxes of vanilla pudding, and a 16 ounce (440 gram) container of whipped topping for a sweet dip.

GIFTING TIP:

THERE ARE MANY DIFFERENT WAYS TO WRAP DIP MIXES FOR PRESENTATION. JARS AND PLASTIC BAGGIES ARE CLASSIC, BUT YOUR PRESENT'S PACKAGING SHOULD BE AS GREAT AS THE PRESENT ITSELF. TRY USING TEST TUBES, CLEAR ORNAMENTS, OR LIGHT BULB-SHAPED JARS. TEA TINS, CRAFT ORGANIZER BOXES, PILL BOXES, AND WELL-WASHED PERFUME BOTTLES WORK WELL TOO.

Onion Soup Mix:

¾ cup (175 mL) minced dried onion flakes

1/3 cup (80 mL) beef bouillon powder

4 teaspoons (20 mL) onion powder

1 teaspoon (5 mL) paprika

¼ teaspoon (1.2 mL) celery seed

¼ teaspoon sugar

Instructions:

Stir into soups and sprinkle over roasts and vegetables. Mix with sour cream and mayonnaise for an easy chip dip.

Made With Loaf

Freshly baked bread is the ultimate homemade scent. Raise your friendship level with a hand-kneaded loaf.

What You'll Need:

3 cups (720 mL) all purpose flour

2 teaspoons (10 mL) salt

1 teaspoon (5 mL) sugar

1 packet or 2 ¼ teaspoons (32.4 mL) yeast

1 ½ cup (360 mL) water

1. In a large bowl, combine flour, salt, sugar, and yeast.
2. Heat the water in the microwave until it's just slightly warmer than your body temperature. (If it's too hot for you to touch, then it's too hot to use.)
3. Pour the water into the bowl of flour. Stir until everything is combined.
4. Cover the bowl and set in a warm place for 20 minutes.
5. Gently stir the dough again. Set aside for another 30 minutes.
6. Have an adult preheat the oven to 400 degrees Fahrenheit (200 degrees Celsius.) Grease a bread pan with cooking spray before placing the dough in the pan.
7. Cover the pan with plastic wrap. Let rise for 10 minutes.
8. Bake bread for 40 minutes or until the crust is golden brown. Let bread cool completely before slicing.

Compound Butter

Wrap your bread up with its perfect mate—butter! But not just any butter. Blend a stick of softened butter with some simple ingredients for a tasty treat. Shape into a roll for easy slicing or use a metal or silicone mold for fun shapes. Or place butter in a piping bag fitted with a jumbo frosting tip. Pipe butter onto a baking sheet lined with parchment paper. Freeze before packaging.

- Berry Butter—2 tablespoons (30 mL) of jam or preserves
- Garlic Butter—one clove of garlic and 3 tablespoons (45 mL) fresh parsley, finely minced
- Breakfast Blend—1 teaspoon (5 mL) maple syrup, 1 teaspoon cinnamon, and 1/8 cup (30 mL) pecans, finely chopped
- Southwest Spread—1 clove garlic and 1 tablespoon cilantro, finely minced, 1 teaspoon chipotle powder, 1 teaspoon lime juice, and zest from one lime, finely minced
- Turkey Day Topper—¼ cup (60 mL) finely chopped dried cranberries, 1 tablespoon (15 mL) orange zest, and 2 teaspoons (10 mL) orange juice

GIFTING TIPS:

WRAP BUTTERS IN PARCHMENT PAPER OR PLASTIC WRAP FOR SIMPLE PRESENTATION. USE STRING, RIBBON, OR WASHI TAPE TO SEAL THE PACKAGES.

EDIBLE LEAVES OR FLOWERS, SMALL JARS OR CROCKS, DECORATIVE TEASPOONS, AND CONDIMENT CUPS ARE OTHER FUN PACKAGING IDEAS.

PRESS SEVERAL DIFFERENT BUT COMPLIMENTARY FLAVORS OF BUTTERS TOGETHER INTO ONE MOLD FOR A LAYERED LOOK. FOR EXAMPLE, PRESS TURKEY DAY TOPPER INTO THE BOTTOM OF A MOLD. FREEZE UNTIL FIRM. ADD A LAYER OF BREAKFAST BLEND. FREEZE. REPEAT WITH BERRY BUTTER.

Bark Bites

Learn all the tricks to making this sweet treat. Your special someone will never guess that it took just a few drizzles to create this dazzling candy bark.

What You'll Need:

resealable plastic sandwich bags

6 ounces (165 grams) each orange, light green, and dark green candy melts

6 ounces chocolate candy melts

Halloween cookie cutters

1 ½ pound (680 grams) white chocolate candy melts

1. Have an adult fill a pot with water and heat until almost boiling. Remove from heat.
2. Place all candy melts into individual plastic bags and seal. Set bags in the hot water to melt the candy.
3. Line a baking sheet with parchment paper.
4. Remove the bag with orange candy melts from the hot water. Knead the bag to make sure all the candy has melted. Use scissors to snip a corner off the bag. Pipe pumpkin shapes onto the baking sheet.
5. Use the light and dark green candy melts to pipe leaves and vines onto the baking sheet. Let set, about 3 to 5 minutes.
6. Drizzle chocolate candy melts over the piped designs. Let set.
7. Set cookie cutters on the baking sheet. Press firmly to cut through the piped designs.
8. Pour white candy melts inside the cookie cutters. Chill until firm. Once the candy bark has set, unmold from the cookie cutters.

Fresh Fridge Pickles

Send your favorite person a "dill"-ightful jar of sweet pickles.

What You'll Need:

1 tablespoon (15 mL) salt

1 ½ tablespoons (22.5 mL) sugar

12 black peppercorns

½ teaspoon (2.5 mL) mustard seed

4 large cloves of garlic, chopped

½ cup (60 mL) white vinegar

1 tablespoon fresh or dried dill

1 large English cucumber (or four small pickling cucumbers), sliced

3-inch (7.6-cm) wide ribbon

hot glue

string

1. Place all ingredients in a large mason jar.
2. Add warm water, leaving the top 1 inch (2.5 cm) of the jar clear.
3. Screw the lid tightly onto the jar. Shake until the sugar and salt are fully dissolved.
4. Let sit in the refrigerator for at least 24 hours before eating.
5. To dress your jar for gift giving, wrap the thick ribbon around the middle of the jar. Glue into place.
6. Wrap the string around the ribbon and tie in a bow.

GIFTING TIPS:

THERE ARE MANY MORE WAYS TO DRESS UP A MASON JAR. TRY SOME OF THESE GREAT VARIATIONS:

- PLACE A CUPCAKE LINER BETWEEN THE FLAT LID AND SCREW CAP.
- WRAP THE ENTIRE JAR IN A TEA TOWEL AND TIE SHUT WITH RIBBON.
- COVER THE ENTIRE LID WITH FABRIC AND TIE WITH STRING OR RAFFIA.
- DECORATE THE OUTSIDE OF THE SCREW CAP WITH WASHI TAPE.
- USE STICKER PAPER TO CREATE PERSONALIZED LABELS.

Taste Bouquet

Dip your hands into the world of edible bouquet making. It's never been easier. A few fruits and some simple tools are all you need to send a sweetly-scented centerpiece.

What You'll Need:

strawberries

skewers

pineapples

cookie cutter

semisweet chocolate chips

mini chocolate chips

floral foam

colored pot or container

tissue paper

Strawberry Roses:

1. Wash strawberries well. Insert a skewer into the leafy end of a strawberry.

2. With an adult's help, use a knife to cut "petals" into the strawberry, about 0.25 inch (0.6 cm) from the bottom. Angle your cuts toward the strawberry's center. Don't cut all the way through. Use the knife to gently bend each petal out.

3. Cut another row of petals above the first row. Stagger the petals' placement so they overlap each other.

4. Continue until the entire strawberry looks like a rose.

5. For variety, turn half the strawberries into roses. Dip the rest in melted chocolate.

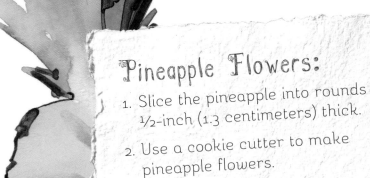

Pineapple Flowers:

1. Slice the pineapple into rounds ½-inch (1.3 centimeters) thick.

2. Use a cookie cutter to make pineapple flowers.

3. Slide a skewer into each pineapple shape.

4. Dip in melted chocolate, if desired.

COOKING TIP:

ORANGES, WATERMELON, MANGOES, CANTALOUPE, HONEYDEW, OR FIRM PEARS ARE GOOD ALTERNATIVES FOR SOMEONE WHO DOESN'T CARE FOR, OR IS ALLERGIC, TO PINEAPPLE.

Grape Sticks:

1. Thread grapes onto skewers. Be sure to leave the bottom few inches of the skewer uncovered.

Apple Wedges:

1. With an adult's help, cut apples into wedges.

2. Slide a skewer into each apple wedge.

3. Dip wedges into melted chocolate.

4. Sprinkle wedges with mini chips while the melted chocolate is still wet.

Dipping Fruit:

1. Place chocolate chips in a microwave-safe bowl. Microwave for 30 seconds, then stir. Continue microwaving and stirring until completely melted.

2. Pat fruit with paper towels to remove as much moisture as possible.

3. Use skewers to dip fruit in chocolate. For the best presentation, dip only half of the fruit.

4. Set dipped fruit onto a baking sheet lined with wax paper. Refrigerate until the chocolate is firm, at least 30 minutes.

To assemble your bouquet:

1. Cut floral foam to fit inside the pot or container, if necessary.

2. Cover foam with tissue paper.

3. Assemble fruit skewers into a bouquet. Trim skewers with scissors to create depth and balance.

83

Powdery Pillows

Show your marsh-fella (or marsh-friend) you're stuck on them with a package of sweet snow white marshmallows.

What You'll Need:

3 tablespoons (45 mL) unflavored gelatin

1 tablespoon (15 mL) vanilla extract

2 cups (480 mL) sugar

½ cup (120 mL) evaporated milk

1 ½ cup (360 mL) powdered sugar

½ cup corn starch

1. Coat a rimmed baking sheet with nonstick cooking spray. Line the sheet with parchment paper. Then coat the parchment paper with more cooking spray.
2. In a large mixing bowl, combine ½ cup water, gelatin, and vanilla. Set aside.
3. In a large pot, combine sugar, evaporated milk, and ¼ cup (60 mL) water. Have an adult whisk over low heat until the sugar is completely dissolved.
4. Increase heat and bring mixture to a gentle boil. Let mixture boil for 12 minutes. Do not stir.
5. Have an adult pour the sugar mixture over the gelatin. Use an electric mixer on low speed until the gelatin and sugar are incorporated. Increase mixer speed to high and beat for 10 to 15 minutes until the mixture is fluffy and white.
6. Quickly scrape the mixture onto the baking sheet with a spatula coated in cooking spray. Spread the mixture evenly. Let set overnight.
7. Mix powdered sugar and corn starch. Use a sifter to dust the top of the marshmallows.
8. Use a pizza cutter to cut marshmallows into squares. Coat marshmallow squares with more powdered sugar and corn starch.

GIFTING TIPS:

Stack marshmallows in clear gift bags and tie the tops with ribbon.

Package with hot cocoa mix or with graham crackers and mini chocolate bars.

For extra decoration, dip marshmallows in sugar sprinkles, color with food coloring, or cut with shaped cookie cutters.

Get Well Stew-n

Soothe the sick and feed the hungry with a bowl of hearty chicken soup. This soup can be given immediately or frozen in the jar for future meals.

What You'll Need:

heart-shaped metal cookie cutter

2 large carrots, sliced

½ onion, diced

2 stalks celery, diced

2 teaspoons (10 mL) fresh or dried parsley

1 bay leaf

64 fluid ounces (2 liters) chicken broth

salt and pepper as needed

1 pound (455 grams) cooked chicken, diced

½ cup (120 mL) uncooked pasta in alphabet shapes

1. Use the cookie cutter to turn carrot slices into heart shapes.
2. Add all ingredients except chicken and pasta to a slow cooker. Cook on high for 5 to 6 hours.
3. Half an hour before serving add the chicken and pasta.
4. When the pasta is cooked through, the soup is ready to eat. Carefully pour soup into mason jars. Wrap a tea towel around the jar and secure with ribbon. Package with seasoned crackers.

Simply Seasoned Crackers:

What You'll Need:

one 16 ounce (440 gram) package oyster crackers

2 tablespoons (30 mL) dry ranch dressing mix

1/8 teaspoon (0.6 mL) garlic powder

¼ teaspoon (1.2 mL) dill weed

1/3 cup (80 mL) vegetable oil

1. Combine all ingredients in a bowl or paper bag.

2. Mix or shake to combine.

Friendship Ketchup

Friends let friends double dip, but sharing the love doesn't have to mean one ketchup packet for two people. There's enough for everyone when you make Friendship Ketchup.

What You'll Need:

12 ounces (330 grams) tomato paste

2/3 cup (160 mL) water

¼ cup (60 mL) vinegar

¼ cup brown sugar

¼ cup white sugar

½ teaspoon (2.5 mL) dry ground mustard

½ teaspoon salt

½ teaspoon cinnamon

½ teaspoon allspice

½ teaspoon ground cloves

½ teaspoon cayenne pepper

88

1. In a bowl, combine tomato paste, water, vinegar, and sugars. Whisk until the tomato paste is thinned and the sugars are dissolved.
2. Place mustard, salt, cinnamon, allspice, cloves, and cayenne pepper in a small bowl. Mix well.
3. Pour the spice mixture into the bowl of tomato sauce. Whisk well until combined. Pour into a bottle and refrigerate. Let flavors combine at least overnight before serving.

COOKING TIPS:

FOR A SMOKY FLAVOR, ADD 2 TEASPOONS (10 ML) SMOKED PAPRIKA AND 1 TABLESPOON (15 ML) WORCESTERSHIRE SAUCE.

TO ADD ASIAN FLAVORS, ADD 2 TEASPOONS FIVE SPICE POWDER, 1 TABLESPOON SOY SAUCE, AND THE JUICE OF ONE LIME.

TO ADD A SOUTHWESTERN KICK, USE 1 TABLESPOON CHIPOTLE PEPPERS, 1 TEASPOON (5 ML) CUMIN, AND THE JUICE OF ONE LIME.

Spaghett-Me-Not

Spaghetti is the perfect friendship food. Prepare a big pot, invite everyone over, and see who stops by! There's always room for one more when you're serving Spaghett-Me-Not.

What You'll Need:

1 2/3 cups (440 mL) all purpose flour

2 large eggs

1 tablespoon (15 mL) olive oil

½ teaspoon (2.5 mL) salt

1. Measure the flour and pour it onto a clean work surface. Pile it into a mound and make a well in the center with your hand.
2. Break the eggs in a small bowl and add the oil and salt. Pour the mixture into the flour well.
3. Use your hands to mix the eggs into the flour. Add a little water if the dough seems too dry. Add more flour if it seems too wet.
4. Knead the dough for 3 to 5 minutes or until smooth. Cover the outside with a little more olive oil and then place in a zip-top bag. Let rest at room temperature for at least half an hour.
5. Flour your work surface well. Use a rolling pin to roll the dough as thin as possible. Use a pizza cutter to cut the dough into noodles.
6. Pile pasta in loose nest shapes on a baking sheet. Set out at room temperature for at least 24 hours or until completely dry. Store pasta in an airtight container or jar or until ready to use. You can also freeze single servings of pasta in zip-top baggies.

COOKING AND GIFTING TIPS:

FOR RED PASTA, ADD 3 TABLESPOONS (45 ML) TOMATO PASTE TO THE DOUGH.

FOR GREEN PASTA, ADD 3 TABLESPOONS GREEN VEGETABLE JUICE.

FOR ORANGE PASTA, ADD 3 TABLESPOONS CARROT JUICE.

TO SERVE, COOK PASTA IN BOILING SALTED WATER FOR 1-3 MINUTES.

LOOK ONLINE FOR FREE PRINTABLE LABELS TO MAKE YOUR GIFT LOOK LIKE IT WAS MADE BY A PRO.

Swirly Sweets

This slice-and-bake cookie dough
is a great gift for any holiday.
Switch the colors to match
the holiday, party
theme, or event.

What You'll Need:

1 cup (2 sticks, 240 mL) butter,
room temperature

1 cup powdered sugar

1 teaspoon (5 mL) vanilla extract

¼ teaspoon (1.2 mL) salt

2 cups (480 mL) flour

blue food coloring

½ cup (120 mL) sprinkles

1. Place butter, powdered sugar, vanilla, and salt in a large bowl. Use an electric mixer on medium speed and beat until everything is light and fluffy.
2. Reduce mixer to low speed and add flour a half cup at a time.
3. Divide the dough in half. Set one half aside. Color the other half with blue food coloring.
4. On a lightly floured surface, roll both pieces of dough into a rectangle shape about 9 x 11 inches (23 x 28 cm). Brush the colored dough lightly with water, and then stack the uncolored dough on top. Roll the dough into a log shape. Roll the log back and forth a few times to seal the seam.
5. Pour sprinkles onto a plate and coat the log in the sprinkles. Press lightly to make sure the sprinkles stick.
6. Wrap dough logs tightly in a double layer of plastic wrap. Refrigerate for at least an hour. Dough can also be frozen.
7. To bake, have an adult preheat oven to 350 F (180 C). Unwrap cold dough log and cut into 1/4 inch (0.6 cm)-thick slices.
8. Place slices 1 inch (2.5 cm) apart on an ungreased cookie sheet and bake for 13 to 15 minutes.

GIFTING TIPS:

Write the cookie recipe and instructions onto a recipe card. Wrap the card around the dough log and tie with ribbons.

Stamp a design onto parchment paper. Use the decorated paper to wrap the dough logs. Tie with string.

Just Because

Whether you want to say "I love you," "You're cool," or even just "Hi," these little shapes will send a message that will bring a sweet smile to your recipient's face.

What You'll Need:

¼ cup (60 mL) water

1 teaspoon (5 mL) corn syrup

1 teaspoon unflavored gelatin

1 pound (455 grams) powdered sugar, plus extra for dusting

flavoring extracts or other candy flavorings

five gel food colorings

small cookie cutter

small letter stamps

1. Combine water and corn syrup in a small bowl. Sprinkle gelatin on top and let stand 5 minutes. Microwave for 20 to 30 seconds or until the gelatin dissolves.
2. Pour the gelatin mixture into a large bowl. Add 1 cup (240 mL) powdered sugar. Use a hand mixer on medium speed to combine.
3. Add the remaining powdered sugar a cup at a time. The dough will be very stiff.
4. Dust your work surface with more powdered sugar. Turn the dough out onto your work surface and knead until it's no longer sticky.
5. Divide the dough into fifths. Wrap four dough balls in plastic wrap. Knead extract and food coloring into the fifth dough ball. When colored and flavored to your liking, wrap in plastic wrap and continue flavoring and coloring the other dough balls.
6. Place a dough ball between two sheets of parchment paper and roll to 1/8-inch (0.3 cm) thick. Use the cookie cutter to cut out shapes. Repeat with remaining dough balls. Place the shapes on a baking sheet lined with parchment paper and let dry for at least 24 hours.
7. Coat letter stamps with food coloring to write messages on each shape.

BAKING TIPS:

VANILLA IS A CLASSIC FLAVOR—BUT NOT THE ONLY ONE! SHOP AROUND AT YOUR LOCAL CRAFT, HEALTH FOOD, OR RESTAURANT SUPPLY STORE, OR LOOK ONLINE FOR INSPIRATION. THEN TRY THESE FLAVOR ADDITIONS:

- EXTRACTS: CINNAMON, ALMOND, LEMON, ORANGE, BANANA, COCONUT, STRAWBERRY
- CANDY FLAVORINGS: BLUEBERRY, CHERRY, APPLE, BUBBLE GUM, GRAPE, WATERMELON
- FOOD GRADE ESSENTIAL OILS: BERGAMOT, CINNAMON, GRAPEFRUIT, PEPPERMINT, ROSE

Sharing Baskets

The key to a great gift is a great presentation! Pair your edible gifts with accessories or other delicious treats for the ultimate gift baskets.

Snow Day

Pair a jar of Get Well Stew-n with a couple logs of Swirly Sweets. Wrap the jar in a scarf and the cookie dough in a pair of mittens or warm socks. Include one of your Delicious Dips for a flavor boost. Add a board game, a puzzle book, or another activity to help your giftee keep warm indoors.

A Trip to Italy

Package Spaghett-Me-Not with canned tomato sauce, meats and sausages that don't require refrigeration, olives, and olive oils and vinegars. Add a fresh batch of Made With Loaf to round it out. Accessories such as wooden spoons and kitchen towels bring the theme together.

Picnic Pack

Send your special someone on a picnic with some Fresh Fridge Pickles, a bottle of Friendship Ketchup, and a travel-sized Taste Bouquet. Bundle it in a basket or an insulated lunch tote. Who's bringing the hot dogs?

S'more To Love

Get your sugar rush on by giving a basket of Bark Bites, Powdery Pillows, and Swirly Sweets! Add a can of gel fuel (with a note on adult supervision!) and some skewers—Bark Bites and a hot toasted marshmallow between two warm cookies and you'll never go back to regular s'mores!

Cider Sippers

A bottle of apple cider is great by itself. When you package it with the fixings for the best cider bar ever, it's even better! Caramel syrup, cinnamon-flavored candies, ground cinnamon or cinnamon sticks, and dried orange slices or peels are great add-ins. And don't forget the Powdery Pillows and some pumpkin spice Delicious Dip!

97

From Me To You
Handmade Gifts for your VIP

Don't the most important people in your life deserve the very best? Give them top-tier hand-crafted gifts made by their VIP—you!

100

THANK you

SENDWORTHY STATIONERY

102

smile
stay

POOCH PLAQUE

104

SHINE BRIGHT CENTERPIECE

Send-worthy Stationery

Giving personalized stationery means thank-you notes just got a whole lot more fun!

Notecards:

What You'll Need:

hot glue gun

blank notecards

used dryer sheet

pigment ink pen (or other pen with slow-drying ink)

embossing powder

1. Plug in the glue gun so it can preheat.
2. Wipe the notecard with the dryer sheet. The sheet will reduce the amount of static on the card and give you a cleaner finished look.
3. Write your word across the card. Quickly sprinkle embossing powder over the wet ink.
4. Tap off any excess embossing powder. Use a small paintbrush to dust off any specks that remain.
5. Hold the metal tip of the glue gun as close to the embossing powder as possible. The heat from the glue gun should melt the powder. Move the glue gun across the card's surface until the embossing powder is melted and raised.

Lined Envelopes:

What You'll Need:

envelope

gift wrap

double-sided tape

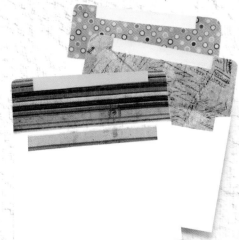

1. Open the envelope. Trace the envelope's shape on the back side of the gift wrap.
2. Cut out the envelope tracing about ¼ inch (0.6 centimeter) inside the traced line. Cut off the bottom ½ inch (1.2 cm) of the liner.
3. Slide the liner inside the envelope with the printed side up. Secure it with double-sided tape.

Pooch Plaque

The perfect gift for your pet-loving VIP—and their Very Important Pet! Tweak the message to fit your recipient's personality, and add as many hooks as you need.

What You'll Need:

picture

wooden plaque

chalk

acrylic paint and paintbrush

metal hook with screws

CRAFTING TIPS:

TURN THIS INTO A JEWELRY OR KEY RING HOLDER FOR THE PETLESS PERSON.

INSTEAD OF A PLAIN HOOK, USE METAL HOOKS, WOOD HANGERS, OR HARDWARE FOR CABINETS.

1. Print out your picture and desired message. Trim the paper to fit on the piece of wood.
2. Color the entire back of the paper with chalk. Flip the paper over and place on the wood. Tape it into place.
3. Use a pencil to trace the picture and letters. Work in sections to avoid smearing the chalk as you trace.
4. Once your letters have transferred to the wood, you can paint them.
5. Once your first section is dry, you can trace and paint the next piece. Continue until your entire picture and message are painted. Let the entire sign dry completely.
6. Screw in the metal coat hook.

Shine Bright Centerpiece

This shimmering centerpiece will both brighten someone's day and reflect well on your friendship.

For the Tea Lights

What You'll Need:

blue glitter

silver glitter

white glue

foam brush

three glass tea light holders

1. Divide glitter into three small bowls:
   bowl 1—all blue glitter
   bowl 2—all silver glitter
   bowl 3—1 part blue glitter, 1 part silver glitter
2. Thin the glue with water so it's spreadable, about 3 parts glue to 1 part water. Brush glue inside the bottom half of a tea light holder.
3. Pour some of the glitter from bowl 1 into the tea light holder. Rotate the tea light holder until all the glue is covered in glitter. Tap out excess glitter. Set tea light holder aside to dry.
4. Repeat steps 2–3 with the remaining glitter and tea light holders.

For the Mirrors

What You'll Need:

paper doily

tape

mirror

frosted glass spray paint

1. Lay the doily over the mirror. When it's positioned how you want it, wrap the back edges around the mirror and tape in place.
2. Spray a coat of frosted glass spray paint over the mirror. Let dry completely, at least 5 minutes or according to the instructions on the can.
3. Remove the tape and doily.

Prop Block

Both the classic cookbook chef and the modern-day digital recipe hunter will flip for this prop block. Whether it's holding up a recipe card or a tablet, it's the perfect cook's companion.

APPLES TO APPLES

INGREDIENTS:

- 1 bottle sparkling apple cider
- 1 cup (240 mL) cranberry juice
- ½ cup (120 mL) orange juice

INSTRUCTIONS:

Stir all ingredients together, and serve. Use red and green cups topped with brown straws to really pull the theme together.

What You'll Need:

wood stain

3 ½ inch (9 centimeter) wood block

3 ½ inch piece of wood molding

medium plinth block

iron-on veneer tape

wood glue

1. With an adult's help, follow the instructions on the wood stain to stain the blocks. Let dry completely before continuing.
2. Decide where the wood block will connect to the plinth block and molding. Lightly mark those areas with a pencil.
3. Have an adult use a craft knife to cut the veneer tape into pieces. Use the tape to decorate the blocks as desired. Do not decorate inside the marked-off areas from step 2.
4. Place a piece of tinfoil over the tape-decorated blocks. Lightly press an iron on the cotton setting over the foil for 8 to 10 seconds. Repeat on the other side of the wood block, if necessary.
5. Connect the blocks and molding with wood glue. Let the glue dry at least 24 hours.

CRAFTING TIPS:

FOR BEST RESULTS, HAVE YOUR DESIGN FLOW FROM ONE BLOCK TO THE OTHER, RATHER THAN HAVING TWO DIFFERENT DESIGNS.

EXPERIMENT WITH A VARIETY OF WOOD STAINS AND VENEER TAPES. YOU COULD ALSO USE PAINT AND WASHI TAPE INSTEAD OF STAIN AND VENEER.

Sugary Snow Globes

You want to bring something special during holiday visits. Look like you went the extra mile with these easy snow globe cookies.

What You'll Need:

cookie cutters

1 teaspoon (5 milliliter) cream of tartar

1 teaspoon salt

1 teaspoon baking soda

5 cups (1.2 liters) flour

1 cup (240 mL) white sugar

1 cup powdered sugar

1 cup butter, softened

2 eggs

1 cup vegetable oil

1 tablespoon (15 mL) vanilla extract

1 teaspoon almond extract

clear hard candy, chopped into small pieces

sprinkles

white, brown, and red royal icing

fruit roll-up

1. Gather a snow globe-shaped cookie cutter and a smaller round cookie cutter. (Or use two round cookie cutters and a trapezoid-shaped cookie cutter.)
2. Stir together the cream of tartar, salt, baking soda, and flour in a large bowl.
3. In another bowl cream together the sugars and butter. Beat in the eggs, then the oil.
4. Slowly beat the flour mixture into the sugar mixture. Finally, mix in the vanilla and almond extracts.
5. Roll the dough out until it is ¼-inch (0.6 cm) thick. Cut out the snow globe and base. Press the two dough pieces together. Use the smaller cookie cutter to cut out the inside of the globe.

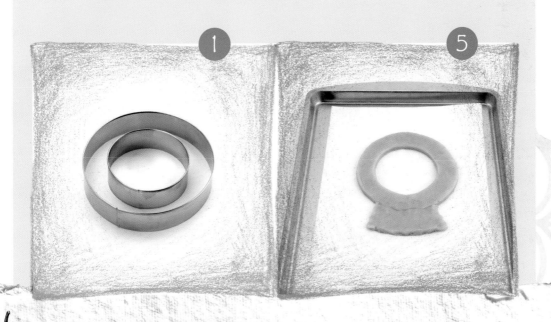

BAKING TIPS:

DISPLAY THE FINISHED COOKIES! USE ROYAL ICING TO ATTACH THE BASE OF THE COOKIE TO A GRAHAM CRACKER. COVER THE CRACKER WITH MELTED WHITE CHOCOLATE OR MORE ROYAL ICING AND A HANDFUL OF SPRINKLES OR SHREDDED COCONUT.

USE MORE ROYAL ICING TO WRITE NAMES ON EACH COOKIE. THEY CAN SERVE AS PERSONALIZED GIFTS OR AS PLACE CARDS.

CONTINUED ON NEXT PAGE

6. Fill the globe with chopped hard candy.
7. With an adult's help, bake cookies for 12 minutes, or until cookies are golden and candy is melted.
8. Decorate melted candy with small white sprinkles. Let the candy harden before moving the cookies onto your workspace.
9. Make and color the royal icing. Divide icing into three separate piping bags.
10. Color the entire outside of the globe with red icing. Start with the edges and then fill in the middle. Use a toothpick to spread the icing, if necessary.
11. Color the entire bottom of the globe with brown icing.

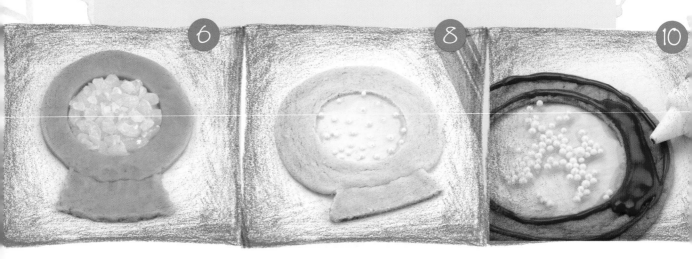

CRAFTING TIPS:

Package cookies professionally by placing in cellophane bags. Use an old curling iron or flat iron to seal the bag closed.

Package unfrosted cookies with sealed piping bags of icing and small containers of sprinkles and candy for a DIY gift.

Use this recipe year-round. Hearts, stars, apples, pumpkins, shamrocks, flags, or even plain circles or squares make pretty cutout shapes.

12. Pipe a white snowman on the candy part of the globe. Let the icing harden for at least 30 minutes.
13. Give the snowman details such as eyes and buttons. Additional details you might want to add are a hat, arms, or pipe.
14. Cut the fruit roll-up into thin strips. Shape a strip around the snowman's neck for a scarf.

Royal Edge Icing

What You'll Need:

2 teaspoons (10 mL) meringue powder

2 tablespoons water

2 to 2 ½ cups (480 to 600 mL) confectioners' sugar

Instructions:

With a mixer on high, blend the ingredients together in a bowl for about four to five minutes. The icing is the right consistency when it forms little peaks that hold their shape.

Memory Box

Whether your VIP likes to travel or you've traveled together and want to collect your shared memories, this gift will be there to capture the moment.

What You'll Need:

hot glue and hot glue gun

two photo frames, one slightly smaller than the other

cardboard

photograph

scrapbook paper

rocks, miniature landscaping figures, or other trinkets

1. Remove the glass and backing from both frames.
2. Use hot glue to attach the smaller frame onto the larger frame.
3. Hold the smaller frame's glass in place with more hot glue.
4. Cut a piece of cardboard slightly smaller than your photo. Glue to the back of the photo.
5. Measure the length between the glass and the larger frame's backing. Cut small pieces of cardboard until you have a stack as thick as the length you measured. Glue all the cardboard pieces together. Then attach the stack of cardboard to the back of your photo. Arrange the photo in the center of the glass.
6. Glue scrapbook paper to the larger frame's backing.
7. Add sand and seashells to the shadow box. Replace the larger frame's backing.

CRAFTING TIP:

YOU CAN ADD ANYTHING YOU WANT TO THIS SHADOW BOX. TICKETS FROM ALL THE PLACES YOU AND YOUR VIP HAVE BEEN TO TOGETHER, TRINKETS, PHOTOGRAPHS, AND OTHER SPECIAL ITEMS YOU WANT TO DISPLAY ARE PERFECT SHADOW BOX ADDITIONS. IF YOU DON'T HAVE ANY SMALL ITEMS, DRILL A SMALL HOLE IN THE FRAME'S BACKING AND ADD HOLIDAY LIGHTS TO ILLUMINATE YOUR PHOTO.

Curious Candy

Mints are the perfect "just because" gift. Your recipient will think of you every time they need a minty treat.

What You'll Need:

ready-to-use gum paste

food-grade peppermint essential oil

gel food coloring

powdered sugar

very small round cookie cutter

1. Break off a handful of gum paste. Knead until it's soft and pliable.
2. Make a small well in the gum paste. Add food coloring and 5 drops of essential oil. Knead until the color is evenly distributed throughout the gum paste.
3. Lightly dust your work surface with powdered sugar. Pat or roll out the gum paste to about 1/8 of an inch thickness.
4. Use the cookie cutter to punch out shapes from the gum paste.
5. Once all your mints are cut out, toss them in some extra powdered sugar to make sure they don't stick together.
6. Spread mints out on a baking sheet and let them dry for 24 to 48 hours. They should be completely dry before packaging.

BAKING AND GIFTING TIPS:

YOU CAN FIND GUM PASTE IN THE CAKE DECORATING AISLE OF CRAFT STORES. FOOD-GRADE ESSENTIAL OIL CAN BE FOUND IN PHARMACIES AND AT HEALTH FOOD STORES.

FOR A CUTE PACKAGE, LAY A PIECE OF FABRIC PATTERN-SIDE DOWN ON YOUR WORK SURFACE. APPLY A THIN LAYER OF DECOUPAGE GLUE TO THE LID OF A METAL MINT TIN. LAY THE DECOUPAGED SIDE OF THE TIN ONTO THE FABRIC. FLIP IT OVER AND SMOOTH OUT ANY UNEVEN AREAS. ONCE THE GLUE IS DRY, USE SCISSORS TO TRIM OFF ANY EXCESS FABRIC.

MEASURE THE BOTTOM OF THE TIN THAT'S NOT COVERED BY THE TIN'S LID. CUT A PIECE OF FABRIC TO FIT. USE DECOUPAGE GLUE TO ATTACH THE FABRIC TO THE TIN. TRIM ANY FABRIC THAT HANGS OVER THE BOTTOM.

Totally Taped

Help your VIP get their thoughts in order with a coordinated set of stationery.

What You'll Need:

plain notebook

white acrylic paint and paintbrush

washi tape

scissors

1. Paint the front of the notebook with acrylic paint. This will help the washi tape stick better, and hide the notebook's color and design. Let dry completely. Repeat with the back side.
2. Starting in the center of the notebook, wrap washi tape at an angle all the way around the notebook. Secure the edges inside the notebook's cover.
3. Use scissors to trim the tape around the edge of the inside covers.

Washi Tape Pencils

What You'll Need:

pencils

white acrylic paint

washi tape

scissors

1. Paint the wooden part of the pencils with acrylic paint. Let dry completely.
2. Cut a piece of washi tape the same length as the pencil. Press tape onto the pencil. Repeat with a second strip, and a third strip if necessary. Trim ends with the scissors.

CRAFTING TIP:

SOME BRANDS OF WASHI TAPE STICK BETTER THAN OTHERS. THINNER OR WAXY TAPES DON'T STICK AS WELL. IF YOUR TAPE STILL DOESN'T STICK WELL, TRY APPLYING A LITTLE CLEAR GLUE TO SEAL THE ENDS.

Style Statement

Giving jewelry as gifts doesn't have to be expensive! Metal washers, which are easily available at hardware stores, can be dressed up to become pretty presents.

What You'll Need:

large metal washers

alcohol ink in three colors

alcohol ink applicator

acrylic gel medium

ribbon

1. Lay washers flat on a newspaper-covered work surface.
2. Dab alcohol inks closely together onto applicator.
3. Use the applicator to sponge alcohol ink all over the washers. Let dry overnight.
4. Turn washers over; repeat steps 2-3.
5. Seal with acrylic gel medium. This will seal the ink's color.
6. Run the ribbon through a washer. Then run the ribbon through a second washer.
7. Thread the end of the ribbon back through the first washer. Pull tight. The washers should overlap each other now.
8. Repeat step 7 until all the washers are used. Tie the ribbon to make a necklace.

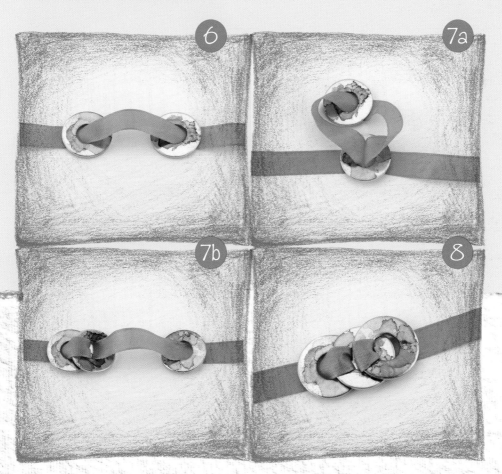

CRAFTING TIPS:

ALCOHOL INK IS A FAST-DRYING TRANSLUCENT DYE THAT CREATES A GLOSSY, POLISHED FINISH. UNLIKE ACRYLIC PAINT, IT CAN BE USED ON METAL WITHOUT PRIMER.

USE THE REST OF YOUR ALCOHOL INK ON CLEAR ORNAMENTS OR OTHER GLASS OBJECTS, COASTERS, OR POLYMER CLAY. YOU CAN ALSO USE IT FOR RUBBER STAMPING PROJECTS AND SCRAPBOOKING.

Fold It, Hold It

Make a simple gift card look like a million bucks with just a piece of paper and a few folds.

What You'll Need:
9-inch (23-cm) square of origami paper

glue dot

1. Place paper color-side down on your work station. Fold in half vertically. Unfold.
2. Fold the sides of the paper in so the edges meet in the center. Unfold.
3. Fold the bottom right corner in so it lines up with the nearest crease line. Repeat for all four corners.
4. Fold the sides of the paper in so the edges meet in the center.
5. Flip paper over. Fold the top of the paper down and crease at the top of the white triangle.
6. Repeat with the bottom of the paper. The edges of the colored triangles should slightly overlap.
7. Insert gift card. Fold paper in half and seal with glue dot.

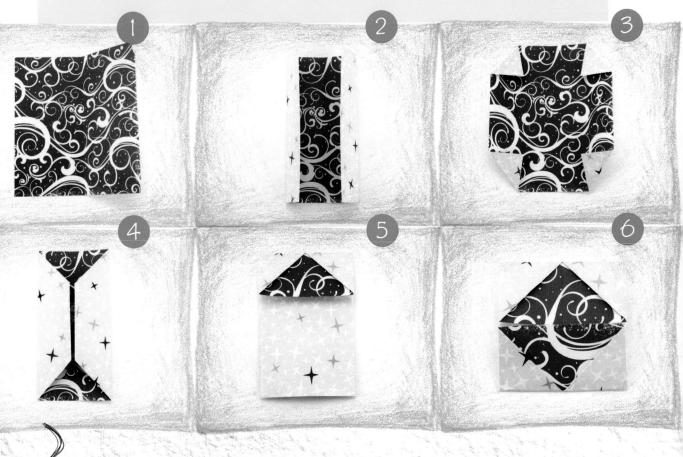

GIFTING TIPS:

THIS MINI WALLET HOLDS MORE THAN GIFT CARDS! SLIP A TEA BAG IN ONE POCKET AND A SUGAR PACKET IN THE OTHER. OR ADD A SMALL PACKAGE OF CANDY FOR AN AFTERNOON TREAT. PHOTOS, MESSAGES, AND DIY GIFT CERTIFICATES ARE THE PERFECT SIZE TOO.

MAKE THE WALLET AS BIG OR AS SMALL AS YOU NEED. OLD CALENDAR PAGES, SCRAPBOOK PAPER, GRAPH PAPER, AND BUTCHER PAPER ARE SOME PLUS-SIZE PAGE IDEAS.

Tick Tock

Remind the hardest worker in your life that sometimes it's nice to slow down. They'll be sure to check the time often with a colorful clock nearby.

What You'll Need:

clock

spray paint

scrapbooking paper

scrapbooking numbers

1. Take the clock apart. You should have the frame, plastic cover, clock hands, battery pack, and paper dial.
2. Spread newspapers on a work surface in a well-ventilated area. Use spray paint to color the clock frame. Let dry completely. Repeat, if a second coat is desired.
3. Use the dial to trace and cut out a piece of scrapbook paper.
4. Glue the scrapbooking numbers onto your new dial.
5. Poke the clock hands through the center of the dial.
6. Put the clock back together.

CRAFTING TIPS:

INSTEAD OF SCRAPBOOK PAPER, USE A PHOTOGRAPH TO MAKE YOUR CLOCK MORE PERSONAL. OR USE SMALL PHOTOGRAPHS INSTEAD OF NUMBERS.

ANYTHING CAN BE A CLOCK! WOODEN PLAQUES, ART CANVASES, PICTURE FRAMES, OLD BOOKS, BICYCLE RIMS, AND CORKBOARD ARE ALL IDEAS FOR A DIY CLOCK. AS LONG AS YOU CAN DRILL A HOLE FOR THE WATCH HANDS, YOU CAN MAKE IT INTO A CLOCK! RECYCLE THE BATTERY PACK AND HANDS FROM AN INEXPENSIVE CLOCK, OR BUY A CLOCK KIT.

Memorable Mittens

Turn a treasured sweater into
an accessory you'll always have
"on hand" as a reminder.

What You'll Need:
knit sweater

chalk

needle and thread

GIFTING TIP:

MITTENS MAKE GREAT PACKAGING FOR GIFTS!
FILL THEM WITH CANDY, COCOA MIX, SMALL
ORNAMENTS, AND OTHER TINY TRINKETS.

1. Turn the sweater inside out. Lay your hand along the bottom hem line of the sweater, with your thumb slightly out to the side. The hem line will be the mitten cuff. Use chalk to trace your hand. Add ½ inch (1.2 cm) all the way around to allow for the seams.
2. Repeat step 1 with your opposite hand.
3. Make loose stitches around the mitten shapes. This will prevent the mitten from fraying when you cut.
4. Cut out the mitten shapes and stack them on top of each other. Sew along the outside of the mitten, leaving the bottom open.
5. Turn the mitten inside out.
6. Repeat steps 1–5 for a second mitten.

Sewing by Hand:

Slide the thread through the eye of the needle. Tie the end of the thread into a knot. Poke the needle through the underside of the fabric. Pull the thread through the fabric to the knotted end. Poke your needle back through the fabric and up again to make a stitch.

Continue weaving the needle in and out of the fabric, making small stitches in a straight line. When you are finished sewing, make a loose stitch. Thread the needle through the loop and pull tight. Cut off remaining thread.

Frosty Friendship

Personalization is an easy way to turn an ordinary present into a VIP gift. Monograms and simple designs are just the start!

What You'll Need:

template
contact paper
craft knife
glassware
rubbing alcohol and cotton ball
craft stick
rubber gloves
etching cream

1. Trace your template onto the contact paper. Use the craft knife to cut out the part you want etched onto the glass.
2. Figure out the design's placement on the glass. Then clean the glass with a cotton ball dipped in rubbing alcohol.
3. Remove the protective backing from the contact paper. Press the design onto the glass. Use the craft stick to press out any bubbles. Be sure that all the edges are completely smooth to avoid etching cream getting under the paper.
4. Put on rubber gloves and use craft stick to apply a thin layer of etching cream over your design. View the design from inside the glass to make sure cream is applied evenly. Let sit for 3 minutes.
5. Use the craft stick to smooth down any etching cream that may have dripped. Let sit another 3 minutes and repeat.
6. Scrape off any excess etching cream. You can place this back in the original bottle to reuse later. Rinse the glass in a steel sink. Once all the etching cream is washed off, you can remove the template.

CRAFTING TIPS:

DO NOT RINSE IN A PORCELAIN SINK. THE ETCHING CREAM COULD DAMAGE THE SINK.

PRACTICE MAKES PERFECT! TEST YOUR TECHNIQUE ON OLD JARS OR BOTTLES BEFORE WORKING ON YOUR GIFT GLASS.

CASSEROLE DISHES, PICTURE FRAMES, AND BOTTLES ALSO MAKE NICE ETCHED GIFTS. USE ETCHING CREAM TO MAKE SPICE JAR LABELS, MONOGRAMMED BAKEWARE, AND OTHER PERSONALIZED KITCHEN GADGETS.

Pretty Packages

Here are more wrapping ideas to make your gifts shine inside and out. From basic bows to do-it-yourself gift bags, you'll never be caught short without a way to wrap again.

Thanks A Million

Being a great receiver is just as important as being a great gifter. Saying thank you is an important way to let someone know you received (and liked) their gift. Here are some tips on how to write a heartfelt thank-you note.

- Record gifts when you get them. Whether you make a list on a sticky note, text it to yourself, or write it in a card, it's important to remember who gave you what.
- Write thank-yous as soon as possible. That way, the gift (and who gave it) is still fresh in your mind. Send thank-yous out within two weeks of receiving gifts.
- It seems like a little thing, but spelling someone's name is a big deal. Double check if you're not sure.
- E-mail is great, but hand-written messages send the biggest impact. Send your thank-yous out on nice stationary and use your best handwriting. If you make a mistake you can't fix, start over. Sometimes it helps to type your message out first. Then you can proofread it for typos or repeating text.
- Add details to personalize your thank-you note. Instead of, "Thank you for the gift. I like it!", try, "Thank you for the stationary set. I'm using it right now!" or, "I loved the cookies you sent. Can we make them together next time you come over?"

Gift Box

Make your gift a true
mystery by hiding its shape
and size in a great gift box.

1. Open the box tabs. Then cut down the center of the box to make a flat piece of cardboard.
2. Fold the box in half horizontally. Unfold.
3. Fold the bottom portion of the box in half.
4. Cut four lines from the top of the box to the fold line from step 2. Cut along the fold line to remove two rectangles from both ends.
5. Make cuts on both sides of the box's back, stopping at the fold line from step 3. Cut along the fold line to remove two squares from both ends.
6. Fold the center piece of the box in half horizontally. Trim the rectangles on either side of the center piece so the top is even with the fold.
7. Flip the box over so the printed side will be on the inside. Fold all four sides of the gift box in. Glue the tabs down.

Gift Bag

With a few fast folds, you can create a gift bag worthy of holding your handmade gift.

What You'll Need:

two 12 inch (30.5 cm) square pieces of scrapbook paper

3 by 6 inch (7.6 by 15.2 cm) piece cardstock

glue

hole punch

ribbon

1. Lay one piece of paper flat on your work surface, print side down. Fold the top edge of the paper down 2 inches (5 cm). Do not unfold.

2. Flip the paper over. Fold the sides and bottom of the paper in 3 inches. Unfold.

3. Make two 3-inch-long cuts along the bottom fold.

4. Repeat step 1 with the second piece of paper. Cut two 3-inch squares off the bottom corners.

5. Trim a tiny bit off two sides of the cardstock. Glue it to the bottom tab on the second sheet of scrapbook paper.

6. Place more glue on top of the cardstock. Place sheet 1 on top of the cardstock. The center tab should line up with the cardstock.

7. Fold the tabs from sheet one under the bag and glue in place.

8. Fold one side of the gift bag up. Apply glue to the outer tabs. Fold the second side of the gift bag up and press the tabs together.

9. Use a hole punch to make two holes at the top of your bag. Thread ribbon through the holes and tie knots to keep the ribbon in place.

Gift Tags

Go beyond generic stickers and folded-over pieces of wrapping paper with a simple yet impressive gift tag.

Chalkboard Tags

What You'll Need:

large paper or label punch

black cardstock

silver permanent marker

white chalk

tissue

white gel pen

small round hole punch

1. Punch out tags from the cardstock.
2. Carefully trace the permanent marker along the edge of the tag, leaving a small edge of black.
3. Rub the flat edge of the cardstock with chalk. Rub off excess chalk with a tissue.
4. Use the white gel pen to write your message. Punch a hole in the tag.

Tie-Dye Canvas Tags

What You'll Need:

canvas sheet

permanent markers

medicine dropper

rubbing alcohol

scissors

1. Protect your work surface with newspaper or paper towels. Cover the canvas sheet completely with the markers. No designing is necessary. Just use a variety of bright colors.
2. Use the medicine dropper to drip rubbing alcohol over the canvas. The alcohol will cause the marker ink to run together. Do not move or tilt the canvas. Let dry completely.
3. Cut out a gift tag shape (or use a label punch.)

Sparkling Tags

What You'll Need:
kraft paper gift tags

gold or silver permanent marker

decoupage glue and foam brush

glitter

1. Color the edges of the gift tags with permanent marker.
2. Paint about one-third of the gift tag with decoupage glue. Sprinkle glitter over the wet glue. Let dry completely.

Photo Tags

What You'll Need:
photo printed out on printer paper

cardstock.

1. Cut the photo and cardstock into 2 x 3 inch (5 x 7.6 cm) rectangles. Glue the photo onto the card stock and let dry completely.
2. Punch a hole in the tag. Trim two corners of the card at an angle for a more finished look, if desired.

Ribbons and Bows

A beautiful bow is the true icing on the cake when it comes to packaging.

Basic Bow

What You'll Need:

thick and thin ribbon

fake flowers

1. Measure about an arm's length of the thicker ribbon. Use your thumb to hold the ribbon at the center of the gift. Then fold the roll of ribbon toward you.
2. Wrap the tail of the ribbon around the package. Tuck the tail under the ribbon fold.
3. Wrap the roll of ribbon under and around the package. Cut the roll of ribbon so it's even with the ribbon tail.
4. Tuck the cut end under the ribbon already wrapped around the package. The ribbon should be snugly wrapped around all four sides of the package.
5. Loop both ribbon ends around each other. Fluff the ribbon and make the tails even.
6. Wrap the thinner ribbon under the large bow and tie into a smaller bow.
7. Trim the ribbon ends at an angle. Tuck the fake flowers through the ribbon knots.

Tulle Topper

What You'll Need:

tulle strips in two different colors

scissors

1. Measure and cut six tulle strips long enough to go around your package and to tie a bow. Stack the strips on top of each other.
2. Place the package in the middle of the tulle. Wrap the tulle around the gift and tie into a bow.
3. Cut the bow's loops. Trim the bow's tails to the same length, if necessary.
4. Pull apart the layers of tulle and gently fluff.

What You'll Need:

scrapbook paper

craft knife

clear tape

1. Type and print out your gift message on regular printer paper. Choose a bold font and use all caps.
2. Cut the words out. Cut strips from the scrapbook paper that are about twice as tall as the words. Decide how you want your message to appear.
3. Center the words on the scrapbook paper strips. Use small pieces of tape to keep the printer paper in place.
4. With an adult's help, use the craft knife to cut around the words. Do not cut out the bottom of the letters.
5. Remove the printer paper and tape. Gently fold the letters so they pop off the scrapbook paper.
6. Loop the paper strips and use tape to secure the loops. Arrange the loops in your desired message. Then attach the loops to your gift. Use ribbon to secure the loops and to hide any paper seams.

Curled Ribbon Bows

What You'll Need:

curling ribbon

scissors

1. Cut a 12-inch (30.5 cm) piece of ribbon. Open the scissors and place the ribbon between the blade of the scissors and your thumb. Run the scissors along the length of the ribbon to curl.
2. Repeat until you have 10 pieces of curled ribbon.
3. Use a small piece of ribbon to tie the curled ribbons together into a bow.
4. Wrap a long piece of ribbon once around your package and secure with tape. Repeat with another piece of ribbon going the opposite way.
5. Place bow on the package where the ribbon pieces meet. Tape in place.

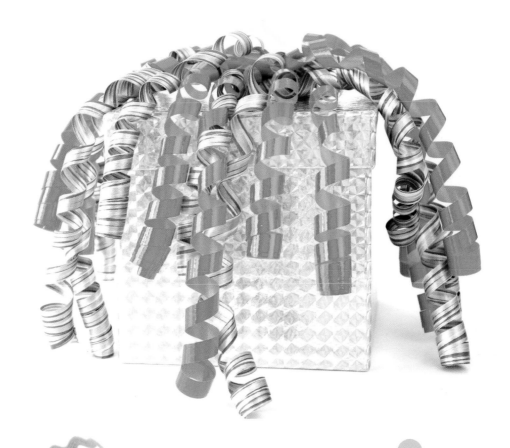

Take A "Bow"

What You'll Need:

newspaper

glue

1. Cut a strip of paper 8 inches
   (20.3 centimeters) long and
   ¾ of an inch (2 cm) wide.
   Repeat until you have eight strips.
2. Fold a strip in half the short way. Then unfold.
3. Twist the ends of each paper strip toward the center,
   to make a figure-8. Glue the ends to the center. Hold until
   the ends are set. Repeat with the remaining strips.
4. Stack three of the folded strips on top of each other
   to create a flower pattern. Glue the strips together.
5. Fold the remaining strips inside the flower. Overlap each
   strip slightly to create more petals. Let the bow dry
   completely before use.

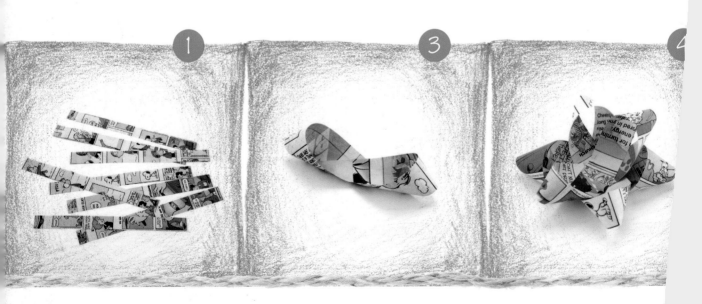

FUN & FABULOUS CRAFT AND ACTIVITY TITLES

for teens and tweens

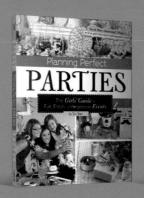

Capstone Young Readers are published by
Capstone, 1710 Roe Crest Drive, North Mankato,
Minnesota 56003.

www.capstoneyoungreaders.com

For information regarding permission, write to
Capstone, 1710 Roe Crest Drive, North Mankato,
Minnesota 56003.

Library of Congress Cataloging-in-Publication Data
Bolte, Mari, author.
  Make it, gift it : handmade gifts for every occasion
/ by Mari Bolte.
      pages cm.—(Capstone young readers.
Craft it yourself)
  Summary: "Step-by-step instructions, tips,
and full-color photographs will help teens and
tweens create personalized presents"—Provided
by publisher.
  ISBN 978-1-62370-319-6 (pbk.)
1. Handicraft—Juvenile literature.
2. Gifts—Juvenile literature. I. Title.

  TT160.B653 2016
  745.5—dc23   2015015952

Printed in the United States of America in
North Mankato, Minnesota.
082015   009133R

Designer: Tracy Davies McCabe
Craft Project Creator: Marcy Morin
Photo Stylist: Sarah Schuette
Art Director: Kay Fraser
Premedia Specialist: Kathy McColley

Photo Credits:
All photos by Capstone Press:
Karon Dubke

Artistic Effects:
shutterstock